Published by Child Care
Marketing Solutions LLC

PO Box 3107
Crested Butte, CO 81224

www.childare-marketing.com

First Edition, 2016

Printed in the United States of America

TESTIMONIALS
FOR THE ULTIMATE CHILD CARE MARKETING GUIDE AND CHILD CARE MARKETING SOLUTIONS

I devoured this book! Not full of fluff, but concise and to the point. It took me about an hour to read (and that was with 3 kids running around after school while my spouse was on a business trip!). The author gives very relevant examples and quick action items that anyone can follow and implement immediately, regardless of your staff size or complexity. The book covers everything from hiring and training (and how to find those 'A' players) to staff retention and knowing when to let the bad eggs go. There is even a list of thought provoking teacher interview questions that will help weed out the potential bad candidates and then a 90-day staff retention plan to ensure that we are nurturing the candidate and not just sending them into a classroom unprepared.

Great for the new and seasoned owner/director alike!!! This will be a great addition to my leadership library for quick reference and refreshing ideas when I need to review. Thank you for this resource Ms. Johnsen!
– Ted C., Lakewood, Florida

This book has an amazing amount of information on the hiring process and beyond. Jessica covers a lot of the background aspects of staffing and retaining employees and clearly ties it together with other parts of the process throughout the book. As a retired childcare director, I wish I had had this resource when I was working. As it is, I am totally passing this book onto the current director for her study. Thanks for pulling this information together in one easy to read resource. I highly recommend it.
– Jane T.

Terrific resource for any manager/owner in the child care business. As someone who has managed a number of schools for a number of years, I can attest to how challenging staffing a child care center can be. And while the book is very practical and thorough in explaining the nuts and bolts of identifying, attracting, screening and interviewing new teachers, the book really hits its stride when it discusses the importance of the school's culture is solving the staffing challenge. It really hammers home that you have to run a school where good teachers want to work and explains concisely what that means and how to manage just such a workplace. We've got a director's meeting scheduled for next week, and there are a couple of sections in this book that we're going to discuss as a group and hopefully implement a few new procedures to help us improve. It's a quick read but very thorough. I highly recommend it.

– Tripp C., Tampa, Florida

This book is easy to read and the author makes it easy for you to apply what you have learned right away. I also noticed the author gives you titles to other books that may go further into detail (if you have the time). Otherwise the action plans at the end of each chapter help you along the way. It has given me a much clearer picture on staffing in my center and I am also including most of these strategies in my business plan.

– Tonya

The Ultimate Child Care Staffing Guide has great nuggets of information given in a fun way. I have taken many valuable tips to improve our quality of staffing along with keeping people long term. I love the quick read format as it kept me engaged throughout the whole book.

– Racheal F., Michigan

Our life since attending Kris Murray's child Care Success Summit has changed immensely both with our business and our personal life! We joined the Gold Program in Kris's Child Care Success Academy and are amazed at the amount and variety of content. Kris and Jessica have helped us become proactive rather than reactive and we have accomplished some great things in our business as a result.

Thank you Kris and Jessica for providing the support we needed to move our business forward and better serve our community. We now have hope for the future instead of just trying to survive day to day!
– Joe and Lucy L., Menomonie, Wisconsin

Kris Murray has been a life saver and such awesome support. Not only have I received the help we needed to take immediate steps to "get the word" out and toot our horns but I have watched Kris' understanding of our industry grow until there isn't a question any of us could have that she won't get an answer for!

Kris knows how many hats we wear. She knows our struggles. Jessica, as a prior program director, knows first-hand how to plug in those supports each of us need. Hats off to Child Care Marketing! Hats off to my staff at The Learning Circle. We've been in business for 31+ years. Together we are making it!
– Michelle H-J., Kirtland, New Mexico

THE ULTIMATE CHILD CARE STAFFING GUIDE

BY JESSICA JOHNSEN

This book is dedicated to everyone who is enriching the lives of children each and every day. Because of each of you, the world is a better place.

I would also like to dedicate this book to my parents. I wouldn't be anywhere in this world without their continuous support on my best days and on my worst. My mother who is my constant rock of strength and my father who reminds me to keep it light and make it a party.

To Priscilla Patti who taught me the importance of relationships. Her motto is "to always do your best, and let others do their best too."

And finally, to Kris Murray, thanks for inspiring me on a daily basis and most importantly, thank you for saving the ripped up paper with my contact information. I am so lucky to get to work with you!

Thank you and I love you.

TABLE**OF**CONTENTS

INTRODUCTION

I went to college to be an accountant, which was a far cry from my childhood dream of being a teacher, or an actress. When I asked my parents if I could switch to Human Development and Family Studies (HDFS) my sophomore year of college they were less than amused that I would switch my major at an out-of-state college, especially to something that would never earn me the income a CPA would. I switched from accounting to marketing, and added HDFS on the side, a fun second major to keep me sane.

Truth be told, I really enjoyed my marketing major as much as I did HDFS, but as soon as I started working at the lab preschool I knew that I was sold in early childhood. Against everyone's advice, I chose to keep working at the Early Childhood Center after I graduated instead of pursuing a career with my business degree. I knew I would use that knowledge as I worked my way up at the center. I made a conscious decision that I had the potential to make far less money, but make a much bigger difference.

I worked at the lab preschool as a teacher and assistant director with director qualifications, eventually becoming a site director. My favorite part about working at the lab preschool was that I got to work with children and college students. About five years later, I met Kris Murray at a conference. She was the perfect mix of my two passions! A year after that, Kris called me up and invited me to her conference in Denver. In 2014, I joined Kris Murray in her journey to help child care owners with best business practices so they could continue to offer high quality care to children all over North America and even abroad.

I set out to write a book about staffing after hearing countless questions about staffing over the past couple years. Because I had the privilege of hiring and training so many college students, it was easy for me to apply those lessons with the stories I've heard from hundreds of owners. Combining that with many many books on leadership, and there does seem to be a clear approach for hiring and keeping wonderful staff at your schools.

With that said, there is a nationwide shortage of job applicants right at the time of this publication. Because of the unique situation you have as a child care owner and/or director, in that you have to keep ratios and children safe, it is much harder to wait to find qualified staff. When you don't have the luxury to wait for wonderful applicants your team is often transient and needs extra training, morale building, and motivation. This creates a cycle of hiring, training, firing, and exhaustion.

If you find yourself in that cycle, it's time to stop. Even if you're just struggling with one or two of those issues, you should find some nuggets in this book to help your processes. This book is designed for single or multi-site owners who want to find a way to have the happiest staff possible. It is designed for those who don't know where to look to find qualified applicants. It is designed for those who aren't sure how their once fantastic employees have now checked out. Even if you take away even one new idea or a little motivation, the world will be better for the children.

My approach to working with adults is much like it is with working with children. Everyone is ready to learn and grow at their own pace. It is a process. Humans are more eager to learn when they are faced with a situation that they need help with. You cannot force learning, opinions, or knowledge onto anyone until they are ready to receive it. The action items at the end of each chapter are designed to start your process, to get you thinking. You will not be able to implement everything at once. Start the process, either in a journal or on your computer, and then prioritize what you need to do immediately.

Teachers and child care staff of high quality programs are the most important people in the world, but so often not recognized as such. I remember being in a classroom so long that the urge to go to the bathroom would go away! I would forget to eat lunch, and then shove whatever was closest and easiest into my mouth, usually lacking any nutritious value at all, it was for energy. It is a hard lifestyle and combined with lower salaries, it can sometimes seem impossible. At the end of the day, small triumphs as children learn something new or master a task they've been working on makes it worth it. It is our jobs as leaders to have the right people in place with motivation so that the accomplishments of children are met with appropriate praise.

I hope you enjoy reading The Ultimate Child Care Staffing Guide, just as much as I have enjoyed writing it. I will refer to my employer and mentor, Kris Murray throughout the book. If you haven't yet, check us out at child care-marketing.com. We work with child care professionals everyday on these topics as well as how to run your centers and keep them full. Kris is the one who started the company Child Care Marketing Solutions who made it all possible to come together as early childhood leaders to find best practices for owners, leaders, families, staff, and children.

JESSICA JOHNSEN
April 2016

FOREWORD

Every once in a while, fate plays its hand and brings someone into your life that can change everything...for the better. For me, that person is Jessica Johnsen. One thing I know for sure is, when I signed up to be a trainer at the Rocky Mountain Early Childhood Conference back in May 2011, the very best thing that happened to me was when a young perky gal approached me after one of my sessions and shyly introduced herself. She basically said "you're doing what I want to do when I grow up." Jessica had the rare combination of co-degrees in both early childhood education and marketing, and she was born to do the work we do here at Child Care Marketing Solutions.

That day, I asked her for her contact information so we could keep in touch. I knew at that point that I'd soon be trying to move back west to Colorado, and there was just "something about her." Have you ever had that feeling? Anyway, she quickly scribbled down her information on a poorly ripped half-slice of notebook paper and handed it to me. Fate had played its hand, now it was up to me to actually keep the paper scrap and be able to dig it out when I needed her to come back into my life.

I'm known around the office as a "piler, not a filer" so it was very unusual – and serendipitous – to be able to access Jessica's information about a year later when I realized my very first Child Care Success Summit event would take place in Denver, near her home base in Fort Collins. I thought she would be the perfect event "helper" to handle registration, microphone running to the audience, and other assorted tasks. Little did I know that her smile and infectious energy at the back of the room would radiate its way into my heart, and inspire me to give literally all I could give at that first Summit conference in 2012.

When I called her that day, she was on the playground of her preschool, watching children and trying hard not to "freak out" with excitement that I was calling. Jessica is an excellent preschool teacher (kids adore her), and quickly moved up the ranks at the ripe old age of 22 into the role of Assistant Director and then Acting Director at the Colorado State University lab school, based on the Reggio Emilia philosophy. If you want to hear someone absolutely gushing about Reggio, just ask Jessica!

Jessica went on to work for Child Care CRM software after the Success Summit conference, as I was unable to hire her full-time at that point. One of the greatest joys of my career was to circle back around to her and offer her a full time coaching and sales position in April 2014, and unbeknownst to me, I happened to extend the job offer to her on her birthday.

Over the past two years, Jessica has soaked up all the ideas, strategies, coaching skills, and best practices she can. She's a force for positivity in our company (which happily is one of our core values) and she brings joy and inspiration to our members and clients. She has had this book "inside of her" for quite some time, and I am thrilled to see it on paper so we can get it into your hands and help you with a much-needed issue: how to hire great teachers, find people who have the potential to be great teachers, train them effectively, motivate them to stay, and inspire your team members to help you be the best early childhood program in your market. Bar none.

So read this book with excitement about what possibilities your staff have inside them, where you can lead your high-performing company, and what impact this journey will have on the children and families in your care. Blessings to you, dear reader! And thank you, Jessica, for sharing your vision of team-building and leadership with the world at large. You are a blessing to me.

KRIS MURRAY
President and Founder
Child Care Marketing Solutions

PART ONE
HIRING & TRAINING

CHAPTER ONE
WHY WILL EMPLOYEES WANT TO WORK FOR YOU?

Before you begin your search for great employees, you must first ask yourself, why would a great employee want to work for me? What do I offer that they can't get anywhere else? The answer probably isn't pay, but for some reason, many child care owners and directors think their retention is largely based on pay. No one is in this industry to get rich, especially as a teacher. Teachers and Early Childhood Professionals have other motivators that drive them besides pay. Your job is to look internally to find out what those motivators are and how you can offer them.

PROTIP:
Our clients who know why they are unique and desirable to employees have the best "luck" finding qualified applicants who want to be hired and stay.

Much like parents searching for care, when teachers are looking for employment, they may think that pay is a differentiator. They will think that only if you give them nothing else to compare between your employment and another child care. Money is tangible and can seem like a reasonable way to make a decision if value is not shown. I will tell you that I practically worked for free (I was an intern when I started) and I put in way more than my contracted hours because I LOVED being at the center. When they did hire me on as an assistant teacher, pay rate was not a factor because I would have done anything to be back with the children and the teachers. Of course, as I got older, pay did make a difference, but I scraped by with a smile on my face.

So what is it that makes teachers want to join your team and stay? There are a couple ways to find out. The first thing you can do is secret shop your competitors as a potential new teacher and find out what they are offering as far as pay and benefits. Another way to find out is to survey your current teachers. Find out what makes them come to work day after day. Ask them what their favorite part about working at your center is and what their least favorite part (or top and bottom three reasons). If you make the survey anonymous, you are likely to get some pretty honest feedback.

What made me want to stay at my organization? Why did I work as many hours as possible and eventually work my way up to Site Director? Benefits and gaining experience were part of my decision. I had excellent PTO and paid holidays. We had enough time to get our classrooms ready and ample time around the holidays to recharge our batteries. We also got a spring break. While I was there we did reorganize those breaks so they weren't as appealing, but we didn't lose any teachers. Why? I can hands down say, the center I worked for had an amazing culture. We were all one big family, with everyone going above and beyond to what was best for the families, children, and each other. We had an administrative team who modeled balance, trust, and out of the box thinking. We had enough autonomy to make our own decisions and we were not micro-managed with our time or our classroom.

I have never heard a teacher say that they took the job for the pay. Something else is making them apply and something else is making them accept job positions, whether it is at your organization or somewhere else. And something other than pay, is making them stay. It's your job to find out what that something else is. It is also important to keep in mind when people leave "because of pay," that the employee at some point was okay with the salary, and although things change and they do have to make a living, you want to know what motivates your amazing teachers to walk through the door each and every morning.

No matter how small (or big!) your organization is, if you create a company culture and an environment based on trust, you will be the most sought after place of employment. You will keep employees engaged, around longer and have more applicants than you will know what to do with. You will be able to be selective and offer better service to children and their families.

Professing that you want to have a great company culture and an environment based on trust is easy. Achieving the right culture can take a long time but can be destroyed overnight. Corporate environments are fragile, living things. The key is to select and then live by core values. In the book *Built on Values* by Ann Rhoades, she details the process in choosing company values and how much these values can benefit your organization. While I cannot do justice to Ann, and highly suggest you pick up a copy of the book, I will attempt to sum up the process and the importance of said values.

POSE QUESTIONS

PROTIP: *Our clients who let their values dictate their culture are the most successful at keeping employees and families!*

To begin, you must first look at where you are as a company and where you want to be. Next, take a look at your "Why." Simon Sinek does a great job of summing up what your "why" is in a popular TedTalk as well as in his book *Leaders Eat Last.* Basically, it eloquently (or maybe not so eloquently) states why you do what you do. What makes you get up in the morning? What made you start this company in the first place? With your why in mind and your present and future comparison, think about what you are representing as a company. As Stephen Covey stated in his 7 *Habits*, you must begin with the end in mind.

Think about what you currently stand for and what you want to stand for as an organization. How are you going to get from point A to point B? Are you on the right track? Do you need to make a few adjustments? Or do you need to make a full overhaul because at some point you've gotten off track? Don't worry if the latter is the case. In the world of Child Care, paperwork, subsidy, licensing regulations, government regulation, parents, children, staff, and competitors often push you down a path you don't even realize you're on until it is too late.

DISCOVERY

Kris Murray and I often help our clients discover their current values. Have your current employees tell you what your organization means to them. This can be accomplished at a company-wide staff meeting, or if you're a larger organization, a management meeting. Have everyone shout out words that they believe describe your company and record on a white board or large sheet of paper. After you have a long list of adjectives, give everyone a post it note and ask them to write down their top 3 descriptions from the list of words. Compile the notes and tally the words on the white board. The top 3 -5 words are your current living values. Many people take these words and make them into their core values and mission statement. If you are not okay with these words, you can decide on what you would want instead and what needs to change to alter your company's values and in turn, culture.

INTEGRATE VALUES

Once you know what your values are, post them and live by them. Caution: do not type them up and hang them around your center never to be thought of again. To really have your values lead your culture, you must live and breathe by them. Your values should guide your decisions They should help you hire employees and weed out employees who don't fit with your values. I will go into how to do this in depth in the coming chapters.

As an example, our company values at Child Care Marketing Solutions are:

- Customer First
- Integrity
- Fun
- Optimism

We use these values in everything we do. Anytime we are making tough decisions, the decisions suddenly seem easier when we weigh our options on how they meet our values. These values also come up during our evaluation procedures. Even if we make a mistake, if we can seriously justify our reasoning was based within a company value, we re-evaluate to determine if it was actually a mistake or if we have a process that needs to be changed.

Another company that has amazing values-based culture is Southwest Airlines. One of their values is also (clearly!) fun. If you have ever flown Southwest, you can tell this is a value by the way their employees clearly love their jobs. They are smiling and helpful and represent the company well. Because of this Southwest keeps their customers over and over again, even when there are small whoops on their flights.

The last time I flew Southwest, I was supposed to stop, but not have to change planes. After the passengers de-boarded, 30 of us were "flying through," and the flight attendant came on the intercom and said "We are so terribly sorry for the inconvenience, but we actually do have to switch aircrafts. As luck would have it, the only place for the other plane is at gate C33 which is on the other side of the airport." The attendants then led us off the plane and to the next gate, they had TSA agents come with carts in case people couldn't make the walk. For those of us who did walk, an attendant walked with us to make sure we knew where we were going. We were then shown where to stand in order to board the flight first. It was seamless, and not one of the 30 people were upset. I have had much worse experiences with planes being switched. On my way home from that trip, as I was boarding, the man loading the plane with luggage was grabbing car seats to put on the plane. He smiled at us and said "hi everyone, I'm so glad you're here today." Southwest's impeccable culture that makes for happy employees is definitely earning them additional revenue from happy customers.

If you are truly living and breathing by your values, trust should naturally follow. Your values make decisions and evaluation much less subjective. If your employees have bought into workplace values, they should easily be able to see why you make certain decisions and why they are required to do undesirable aspects of their jobs. Does this prevent burn out – perhaps, but at a minimum it should help you assist your staff find work-life balance. Do your values prevent gossiping – nope, but they should guide you on what to do with those who gossip.

The first step is to identify your values, begin living by them, and only then will you be able to create a culture where you have both families and potential staff beating down your door to get in. Assuming you have discovered and implemented your values, let's move on to how to hire amazing staff to also live by your values. As we talk about where to find employees, how to attract them, your hiring process, your training plan, and your retention plan, I will point out how to weave your company values through-out each step.

ACTION STEPS:

- Survey your current employees to find out what made them want to join your team and why they stay with you.
- List your Unique Benefits to employees. What do you offer that no one else currently offers or could ever offer?
- Identify your current values. Have your staff tell you what they think your values are. Are they in line with what you want your values to be?
- Define your "why" or reason for existing.

SUGGESTED READING:

- Read Simon Sineks *Start with Why* and *Leaders Eat Last.*
- Read Ann Rhoades *Built on Values.*

CHAPTER TWO
WHERE TO FIND QUALIFIED EMPLOYEES

If I'm being honest, I went back and forth deciding if "where" should come before "how." Truthfully, I really think the "How" is truly the first step, because if you put this book down after the "where" you will miss a HUGE part of gaining qualified candidates. With that said, many of you are linear and need to know your platform before you can do anything else. Please take this incredibly long first paragraph as a warning – do not put this book down after this chapter. If you do, you will likely not see the results you want, and at that point you will be tempted to write me an email telling me you had no luck with the process. I will then ask you to read chapter 3. There, look at how much time I've already saved both of us, just in the first paragraph. (Can you tell my favorite book as a child was The Monster at the End of this Book?)

Back to the topic – Where should you be looking for qualified employees? Here at Child Care Marketing Solutions we separate candidate search into two main categories: Online and Offline. While we are an increasingly on-line society, we don't want to discount the offline ways that have been working for years.

BE TARGETED IN APPROACH

Before you start reading the list of different places to find very qualified staff, take a moment to think about who you want to attract. Are you looking for an infant teacher who is like a grandmother to everyone and will spend all day patiently loving on the babies enrolled in your center? In that case you may want to check out a local retirement community (not to be confused with assisted living or a nursing home). Many women and

PROTIP: *Know who you want to attract and think outside of the box on where he or she might hang out.*

men in retirement communities may pick up a shift (even an early one) for something to do or some extra money. The other benefit is, if they are like my grandmother, they may pass the job notification on to one of their children or grandchildren.

If you're looking for a great cook, consider advertising at a local restaurant. Wouldn't it be cool if a local chef wanted to pick up extra hours – or an aspiring chef wanted some experience? The point I'm making is don't be afraid to step out of the box and try one or twenty new things.

KEY WARNINGS

Before I start with my lists of where to find qualified candidates, I feel compelled to give you two warnings regarding frequent mistakes.

Caution 1: "Now Hiring" signs on your lawn, on your building, or on your website. Advertising for staff where your parents can see might have a negative impact on current or potential parents. You never want parents to think you are understaffed or getting ready to fire someone. Changing your phrasing to "Always looking for fun team members" or "we never turn away applicants with the desire to change children's lives" sounds much better.

Caution 2: Craigslist is a waning resource. Not only is Craigslist starting to charge, our members have reported it less and less successful. The same goes for newspapers, but again, consider where the person you are trying to attract might hang out.

I'm not saying these resources NEVER work, just don't put all of your figurative eggs in one basket, especially if that one basket is craigslist or the newspaper.

WHAT WORKS

Let's move on to what is working. We will start with online resources, which are often an effective and quick way to start. The nice thing about online resources is that they work for you while you sleep. The internet is always going and web resources are constantly updating information and marketing to people *for* you.

ONLINE:

CAREERS PAGE ON YOUR WEBSITE

The careers page on your website is one of the most important things to have when seeking exceptional candidates. Your careers page should be two-fold. It will help convert candidates who seek you out by searching for your company online; and it can also be a landing page from your other online efforts.

Your Careers page should include:

- Employee testimonials – Nothing attracts people more than social proof. You can talk about how amazing the center is all day long. However, it is more believable when others talk about your center. Have your "A" employees write why the love working for you.
- Core Values – Or excellent copy that portrays your Core Values (see chapter 3).
- Unique benefits – Why you are the best place to work, what differentiates your center and what you offer that your competition may not offer.
- Virtual Tour – If you have this available for parents, put it on this page as well.
- Call to Action – What is the next step potential employees should do to start the process.
- Special Offer – This isn't necessary, but if you are not getting a lot of applicants, it might be worth offering an incentive. Offering to buy them lunch or coffee is a great way to get applicants to send in their applications. "Please submit your application, if we think you might be a good fit, we'd love to buy you coffee to continue getting to know you."

Note: if you get a lot of applicants, you can have more "hoops" for your candidates to jump through (I.e. resume, cover letter, application, references). If you do not get a lot of applicants, consider requesting less upfront. If you just have them send an introductory email, it's much less intimidating to potential candidates. If I am moderately happy at my current job, I will not spend A LOT of time filling out applications or updating my resume. I would be more willing to write a quick email to see if there is a potential fit.

An excellent Careers Page on your website can do a lot of work not only attracting, but also qualifying leads.

Once you have your Careers page you can begin generating traffic to said page. The most obvious places are links with other online resources.

GOOGLE SEARCH/SEO/PPC/ADWORDS

Believe it or not, people start their search for jobs much like they start any other search, on Google. Make sure your Webmaster has your careers page optimized to be found on Google. Use keywords such as child care job, child care jobs, day care job, preschool teacher careers, teacher employment, etc.

It might also be worth your time and money to use pay per click or adwords on Google. I am not going to go into depth on this one, that'd be another book. Your webmaster can explain this easily.

ONLINE RECRUITING WEBSITES:

We recommend using the following:
- Indeed.com – many of our clients have luck using both the paid and unpaid versions of indeed.com. This site (as do the others) really depends on your location for success. Because this is a national site, you may want to have more "hoops" to your application process.

Tip: At the time of this publication, Indeed makes you set a dollar amount as your "Job Budget." Choose $0 as your dollar amount and click on "Keep this job free" at the bottom.

- Monster.com
- ZipRecruiter.com
- CareerBuilder.com
- SnagAJob.com
- Switch – This is a new mobile app which is being marketed

as the "tinder" for jobs. Tinder is a dating app that has grown in popularity. At the time of this population, we have not tested Switch as it is brand new in the market place.

SOCIAL MEDIA

> **PRO**TIP: *Many of our clients have had great success using paid Facebook Ads to find qualified employees. Be sure to set your demographic to target the ages you want.*

Social Media is definitely where the millennials hang out, and it's not just millennials anymore!

- Facebook Ads- Carefully crafted ads on Facebook are driving a lot of traffic to our client's career pages. The beauty here is you can target only your wanted demographic.
- LinkedIn – LinkedIn is designed as a social network for professionals. Join some Early Childhood Education (ECE) groups to find the demographic you're looking for. To date, LinkedIn isn't quite as savvy as Facebook when searching for your exact demographic, but it does attract more professional users.

While online is quick, easy, and can be effective. We don't want to discount offline approaches. They often take more time, but include face to face interactions and unplanned first impressions.

OFFLINE:

COLLEGES AND UNIVERSITIES

There are two ways to seek employees from colleges and universities. The first way to find candidates from a local college or university is to post on their job board. You may have to call their human resources department to find out how to do this. Most colleges have an online posting for part time jobs for which students can apply. Some of these positions qualify for work study and others do not. The nice thing is that many of your part time shifts can be filled by college students who want to make a little income between classes.

You can also contact the career counselors. Many large universities offer students help finding employment. You can post a listing within the career department and they can help match you with interested and qualified candidates.

The other option is contacting the Human Development and Family Studies (HDFS), ECE, or Education departments to determine if you can be a site for supervised internships. This will attract passionate students who are training to be teachers someday. They may also be eager to become full time employees when they graduate.

CAREER FAIRS

These might be held at colleges or universities as well as by your city council. Contact your city council or chamber of commerce to find if they offer any career fairs. A few of our clients have even hosted their own career fairs. This is a great way to make community partners as well. Another benefit is possible cross promotion of employees and clients.

LOCAL RECRUITING FIRMS

These are not as popular in many areas, but some still do exist. Again, your local chamber of commerce or city council will be able to point you in the right direction. Many local recruiting firms have been replaced by online resources.

FLYERS AND SIGNAGE

It is also worth your time to put up flyers and/or signage in places your target employees hang out. As I mentioned earlier in the chapter, think of where your current employees frequent and work with those businesses to see if you can post employment fliers. Some ideas would include gyms, doctor's office, barbershop/salon, apartment buildings, and housing developments.

EMPLOYEE REFERRAL PROGRAM

Many of our clients have been successful offering incentives to current staff members who refer someone for employment. Some centers choose to only reward the current employee if they hire the candidate referred. This may help your employees only refer qualified candidates. In this industry it seems prevalent that people are afraid about being taken advantage of for their referral programs. That might happen if you don't have the right people to begin with. If you give referral rewards to employees just for the applicant, it shows you trust your employee's judgement enough to refer someone they would want to work with and who would benefit the school. It might be worth giving a small incentive for anyone who refers a friend and then a bigger bonus if that person gets hired.

PROTIP: *Employee referral programs are a great way to let your staff do the qualifying for you! Staff will only recommend people they would want to work with.*

Hopefully you've taken away at least one new idea on where to find qualified staff. I want to encourage you to try multiple ways consistently to see what works best for you. Kris always says "to find the most qualified candidates you must be willing to widen your net."

Now we will move on to How to attract "A players." As I mentioned at the beginning of the chapter, you can be looking in all of the right places and still not get qualified candidates if you aren't sending the right message.

ACTION STEPS:

- Decide who you want to hire. How old is the person? Where does the person hang out? How much do they want to work?
- Create or update your Careers Page on your Website.
- Try and search for your job posting online using keys phrases like "jobs in Child Care" or "hiring a teacher."

- Decide what online and offline approaches you want to try first.
- Time block time on your calendar to create job listings and monitor them.

CHAPTER THREE
HOW TO ATTRACT "A PLAYERS"

DEFINE QUALITIES OF "A PLAYERS"

In order to attract "A Players" you must first determine what an "A Player" looks like to you. Is your "A Player" someone older with a lot of experience and gives off the loving mother or grandmother vibe? Is she someone who is fresh out of college, eager to learn and progressive in her ways?

To find out who you want to attract, first look at who your "A Players" are now. What are their strengths? Where do they hang out? What do they do in their free time? What do you really like about them? What makes them great in the classroom? What makes them great outside of the classroom? How do they relate to the parents?

I'm sure you are thinking "it could be any number of things, my "A Players" are all different. This may be true, but a lot of people make the big mistake and go into the hiring process without first identifying what or whom they are looking for. Defining qualities upfront makes your hiring process more objective and less emotional. If you're using a hiring assessment such as Strengths Finder (which we recommend), identify what strengths you are looking for ahead of time.

MAKE ADS SPECIFIC

PROTIP: *Defining qualities upfront makes your hiring process more objective and less emotional.*

Many use generic copy or what we call the "me too" approach. These are not as effective in attracting candidates you desire. These employment ads typically read something like this… "now hiring qualified teachers for our

PROTIP: *You want your ad to be a qualifier in itself to help weed out anyone who isn't a good fit.*

infant room. Must be 18, have CDA, and a desire to work with children. Fill out this application, send a blood and urine sample, resume and cover letter." (Just kidding on the blood and urine sample.)

The key to getting great applicants is to show personality in your ads. You want your ad to be a qualifier in itself to help weed out anyone who isn't a good fit. An example is when Google placed a billboard looking for coders, the phone number to call was in code. So anyone who could figure out the code would call. Not only would Google only attract people who were already qualified with technical skills, but anyone who would spend time figuring out code on a billboard, was likely a passionate candidate as well.

"Are you ready to make a difference in the lives of children, and join a winning team? We are the best early childhood program in the area and we only hire the best. We are always looking to add talented, energetic, positive, honest, and fun people to our team. Young or old, if you have the stuff, we'll know it. Negative people, gossipers, and whiners need not apply. Must be an outstanding communicator and rapport-builder with parents. EXCELLENT wage and benefits, and paid training! Prior early teaching experience a plus, but not required. Send resume, cover letter, and writing sample to apply@ bestchildcare.com."

PROTIP: *You need to have personality and show who you are in your ad.*

This is an ad that Kris often recommends on stage. Many people love the ad, but a few are turned off by "Negative people, gossipers, and whiners need not apply." That's ok! Your ad needs to reflect your center. If you think that's too negative, change it to "only accepting applicants who have a positive attitude and love getting hugs every day." The point is, you need to have personality and show who you are in your ad. I believe in putting what you want out to the universe. So write what you are looking for in your ad. "We love our teacher's positive attitudes and team focus, apply today if you think you'd fit in." If you're a tech focused school, you could try:

We are looking for a fun, motivated individual who can operate a tablet, post on social media, and build self-esteem in four year olds? Think you've got what it takes? All energetic, tech savvy people who love laughing and want to earn competitive wages, please email us at ___."

If you're looking for someone for your infant and toddler room who really has a passion working with your youngest learners, you could use something like this:

Seeking a patient, loving individual who enjoys rocking our littlest learnings and planning both stimulating and soothing activities. Changing diapers is in your job description, but our best candidates will understand what amazing social time it can be! If you're interested in loving on our babies and updating our parents via email throughout the day, please email _____."

A couple notes on the ads above. If they reflect your values, but you think they might scare away potential candidates – good! I wouldn't want to hire anyone for my four-year-old room who didn't have a lot of energy and know how to use a tablet. I also don't want to hire anyone for my infant room who doesn't appreciate the patience and love it takes or understand what a baby is learning developmentally. I always say hire for character and train for skill, but you never, never want to hire anyone you have to convince to love their job. I would rather hire an eager younger teacher who shows desire to learn, than someone with "experience" who might be stuck in their ways. On the other hand, if you have a younger staff or staff

PROTIP:	*Hire for character and train for skill.*

who has been with you for so many years that things are getting stale, it's nice to hire someone amazing with experience at another school to freshen things up.

CLEARLY STATE CALL TO ACTION (CTA)

Tell the applicant how to apply. If you are hiring for a specific position, you may want to give a deadline. Even though you should ALWAYS be hiring, a deadline for a specific position will make people act now. For instance, if I have a job and I see your ad, I might think "hmmm, if I really start to hate my job now, maybe I'll apply someday." If you have a deadline, the person will think "I don't really love my job and I don't want to miss out, I may not have another chance."

PROTIP:	*Even if you do not have a position open, you should always be hiring.*

Like I mentioned, you should ALWAYS be hiring. Even if you don't have any positions available, you still want to be marketing for candidates. You may run a "We are always looking for great team members" ad so you can start collecting resumes and sifting through for your "A Players."

Your CTA should also include how your applicant should apply. If you have a lot of applicants and they're not always qualified, then it is good to have an application for them to fill out, and request a resume and cover letter. If you do not have a lot of applicants take a look at your process. Are you asking too much of your applicants? On more than one occasion, I've seen people asking for social security numbers on the application. I am a person who does not give out my social security number very easily. If I saw that on an application I might pass. I understand that a social security number is necessary for background checks, but that should come after the initial interview.

If you don't get a lot of applicants, you can simply ask candidates to email you. You can tell a lot from an introduction email, i.e. spelling, grammar, and personality. A simple email showing interest is a non-threatening and easy way to get more applicants.

HOW TO HANDLE INTERVIEW NO SHOWS

As silly as it seems, I would also like to address interview no-shows. It always blows my mind that an applicant wouldn't show up for an interview, but unfortunately in this day and age, it occurs. If you have one or two no shows, it happens. Alternately, if you find yourself getting a pattern of people who don't' show up, here are a couple suggestions to help reduce interview no shows:

- Have more dialogue up front. Ask for more information and have more information exchange before you invite someone in to interview. The more time and effort people put in ahead of time, the more serious they are about applying. This doesn't have to be spread out over a period of time, just a few phone calls and emailing back and forth over 2 or more days.
- Confirm the time of the interview. Send the applicant an email confirming the time of the interview. Include a short agenda or what the applicant can expect during the interview.
- Ask the applicant to let you know if they can't make it. Say something like "if for whatever reason you can't make it, please call me at _____ or email me at_____."

PROTIP: *Send an email to confirm the interview and let them know what to do if they have to reschedule.*

- Give the applicant an option or an out. If you sense the applicant is hesitant or unsure, be straight forward. "I think you'd be a good fit here based off what I've heard so far, I'd love to invite you in for an interview so you can see for yourself why our teachers love it here. Do want to schedule something or would you like some time to think about it?" OR "You seem unsure of the pay and I completely understand. I would love for you to come in for an interview and I can show you the numerous other reasons why our teachers love working here. If you know it just won't work, that's ok too, but please keep us in mind for the future."

- If you are still having a hard time getting people to show up, you may want to start recording your phone calls to listen and review. You might hear something off putting in what you say or how you say it. I get loads of perspective listening back to my own calls. I find that sometimes I sound nervous, tired, or too desperate.

TECHNIQUES TO ATTRACT

Again this chapter is about attracting the right candidates. A lot of the same methods we recommend to attract parents will also help you attract employees. Here is a summary check list for attracting employees.

- ◯ Do you have a careers page on your website?
- ◯ Do your current employees sing your praises?
- ◯ Do you have great copy that shows your values and personality?
- ◯ Are you using the right media? (Online & Offline)
- ◯ Is your process too complicated?
- ◯ Is your process not complicated enough?

If you are having trouble answering any of these questions, it would be worth your time to survey current employees about what they did and didn't like about the hiring process.

ACTION STEPS:

- Write out all of your employees and give them a grade, A-F.
- Determine what qualities make your "A" employees an "A."
- Determine what qualities give your C,D, or F employees their grades.
- Replace D, and F players as soon as you can.

- Write an ad with personality defining the characteristics you're looking for.
- Confirm interviews with applicants and give instruction what to do if they can't make it.
- Survey current employees what they liked and didn't like about the hiring process.

CHAPTER FOUR
THE INTERVIEW PROCESS

PRE-INTERVIEW GAME CHANGERS

Think of your interview like you think of your tours. Here at Child Care Marketing, we have coined six steps to do on the tour and those all translate to the interview process as well. As much as you want to hire the right person, you want the right person to want to work for you. Trust me, your "A Players" definitely have options. Here are the 6 Things to remember during the interview.

1. The 5 Senses and Wow Welcome

How does your building and atmosphere greet the applicant? Are there dead plants when they walk in? Broken toys on the playground? Dirty dishes in the kitchen? How does your building smell? Your building and the people in it will be seen as a future 'Home' to the potential applicant. You want to have put your best foot forward.

Sight – If the person sees dead plants or broken toys, it could give the impression you are understaffed or the current employees are lazy or don't care. This screams "stressful environment". I do not want to be hired into a place where employees don't care enough or are too busy to throw away a toy or water a plant. It gives the impression the new employee will be left to pick up the slack.

Smell – Have a candle warmer or an essential oil diffuser going to cover any unwanted smells.

Sound – Children cry and that is expected in the environment. As long as the crying isn't accompanied by a stressed (or even worse, yelling) teacher, it should be ok. Have quiet soothing music going or schedule an interview when you know the children will be having fun, like circle time or free play or even nap time. We all know that our environment can be chaotic, but that isn't the first impression you want to give.

Touch – Make sure you have comfortable, adult-sized furniture to conduct your interview. We have all used those kids chairs, it is not comfortable for a long period of time and will be an unwanted distraction.

Taste – Offer the applicant something to drink at the very least. You can have snack foods such as cookies or cuties available as well. The applicant likely won't take anything, but it's a nice touch. This extra effort lets the applicant know your school is friendly and has those things on hand for parents as well.

2. Ask the Applicant what they are looking for in employment

It is important to know what will provide the candidate with the most satisfaction. Sure, this could be money and benefits, but more often than that you will find it's a safe, happy work environment. Just like we suggest with parents, you could even give the applicant a questionnaire and they can rate aspects that they find important about their job. For instance, you could say:

Please rate the following preferences in order with 1-10, 1 being the most important

1. Hourly Rate/Salary Rate
2. Health Benefits
3. Paid Time off
4. Excellent Co-Workers
5. Team Environment
6. Freedom to implement ideas and activities in the classroom
7. Resources for classroom/school
8. Flexibility with schedule
9. Bonuses/fringe benefits (child care, employee rewards, etc.)
10. Number of hours worked

PROTIP: *Find out what is important to your applicant while seeking employment.*

Much like parents say "safety" or "school readiness" when they are asked what they are looking for, applicants may say "pay" because they don't know what else to say or what the job entails. Once you have listened to the applicant's responses, be very honest on what you do or do not offer. Do not make false promises that you can't fulfill or that your staff won't fulfill, but do let the applicant know what you offer for job satisfaction besides a pay check.

3. Communicate your Differences

Just as you want to stand out to the parent, let the applicant know how you stand out among your competitors as an employer. What do you offer your employees that they won't get elsewhere? Here are some examples of benefits you tell your parents that are benefits to the teachers as well:

Zono – Sanitation machine that keeps not only children healthier, but teachers as well. When fewer children are sick, that means less chaos with call outs and happier children. We've all had that child who is cranky all day and then we find out he or she is running a fever.

Low Staff-Child Ratios – Satisfied parents, less children coming and going, better relationships with the children and families, calmer room and learning environment.

Full with a Waitlist – Less child turnover, fewer cubbies and name tags to make.

Electronic Daily Report (KidReports, LifeCubby, MyChild) – Tablets in every classroom, no written daily sheets, better communication with parents.

Cameras in the Classroom – Reassurance for parents, better protection if a parent complains, helps directors and resources identify children with potential special needs.

Organic Fruits and Vegetables – Promoting a healthy environment for staff and children.

NAEYC Accredited – Higher standards means better work environment for staff and learning for children. NAEYC has a whole standard dedicated to staff and leadership.

If you aren't sure what your unique teacher benefits are, ask your current teachers what they love about working for you. Maybe it's flexible shifts, guaranteed hours, or friendly co-workers.

4. Teacher Connection

It is always a good idea to let teachers sit in on your interviews. Teachers work so closely together it is important for them to start making connections as soon as possible. This process could help identify potential new mentors or co-teachers for applicants. You don't want to have too many people in the interview that you intimidate the applicant, but you want to make sure you have some teachers included in the process.

Caution: Be careful trying to hiring someone "just like me" or "just like ____". Everyone has different strengths to add to the team. No two people think exactly alike. If you hire someone because you think they are "like me" or "like so and so", you will often be disappointed and be holding that person to an unrealistic standard. Know what strengths you want to hire ahead of time to prevent this emotional decision.

5. Give the applicant something to take home

Whether it be a folder of information, a logo'd mug, or a printed copy of your e-packet. This memento of the school provides several benefits. It is a small token of appreciation for taking their time to meet you and a future reminder of how great you are. You want the applicant to be hoping for a job offer when they walk out the door and go home.

6. "Close" the interview

Depending on how strongly you are considering the applicant, different closing actions may be applied. You want to ask the applicant to join your team on the spot. Alternately, let them know the process and timeline if you were to ask them to join your team. If you are considering them, you may want to schedule a time for them to come observe the classroom or for you to observe them in the classroom. Don't discount them observing the room and jump right to you observing them. Many of the best teaching practices I learned were derived from observing other good teachers. Have the applicant watch your best teachers in action so they know your culture and what's expected in the classroom. Then watch them in action. Once they have a feel for the environment, they should be able to comfortably (or somewhat comfortably) enter into the classroom to show you what they've got! Finally, let your applicants know the date on which you plan to make your decision.

THE ACTUAL INTERVIEW

Now that you have the process in mind, let's talk about the actual sit down interview. Of course you want to sell yourself and your school as an amazing place to work. Additionally, you want to make sure you hire the "A Players" we've been discussing in these first four chapters. Here are some ways to help you objectively hire quality employees:

Have Scoring Criteria

Some of the best companies (Southwest, Google) have scoring criteria when hiring. Applicants are scored on their answers to questions and the questions are weighted based on the values of the company. This sounds harder than it is to write. Think of all of the criteria you look for, such as professional dress, hand shake, correct grammar, developmentally appropriate knowledge, experience, education, and friendliness. Have whoever completes your interview process give each criteria a score (can be between 1 and 5 or 1 and 10) and then add up their score. Know what score constitutes a "hire on the spot" or "end interview quickly" and everything in between.

PROTIP: *Ask the applicant what they have done in a situation instead of what they would do.*

Behavior Based Interview Questions

Know your interview questions ahead of time and make sure they reflect your values. Behavior based questions ask the applicant what they have done in a situation instead of what they would do. It is easy to answer a hypothetical question "correctly," but having to give actual examples is much more telling of an applicant's true behavior. We have included example interview questions based on Values in Appendix A.

A favorite question that I like to ask, is "Why are you leaving your current position?" or "Why are you looking to switch jobs?" I have had some major red flags come up with prospective employees who complain or talk badly about a past position. Yes, there are some poor employers out there; however, there are two sides to every story. How the applicant handles this question will tell you a lot about their character. If they talk negatively about past employers, they won't think twice about talking negatively about you some day. If they talk about an opportunity or lessons learned at prior employment in a positive manner, this shows great class.

Know What You Are Looking For

Can you tell this is important? Even though I've mentioned it previously, this deserves re-stating because it is important to keep in mind at each stage of the process. You want to go into the interview knowing what you're looking for. What behaviors, strengths, characteristics do you need the applicant to display to be a great fit with your center or school?

Assess Candidates

We recommend using Strengths Finder when assessing candidates. This assessment is based on the popular book *Now, Discover your Strengths* by Marcus Buckingham. The book is based on numerous studies conducted by the Gallup Institute. Basically the main principle is that all humans have unique strengths and weaknesses. Instead of trying to find well rounded people, we should strive for well-rounded teams. Just as Stephen Covey has "sharpen the saw" as a habit of highly effective people, Buckingham suggests developing people's strengths and merely "doing damage control" on their weaknesses.

All 34 strengths are broken up into four categories: Relationship, Influencing, Strategy, and Execution. My top 5 strengths are within Influencing and Relationship, so my ideal teammates have strategy and execution – that way we will actually get things done!

Have your top candidates Observe and Audition

I talked about this earlier in the chapter, but to reiterate it's important to have candidates observe the classroom. You should also observe your candidates. For both observations there should be set questions and qualities to look for. When your candidates observe have them watch for behavior management, developmentally appropriate practice, parent communication, child/teacher relationship, and teacher-teacher interactions. You should watch for similar criteria when observing.

How your applicant begins to form relationships with children and co-workers will likely be telling of their future interactions. Does the candidate go in and take charge? While this may be seen as great initiative, this can be off putting to the children and disrespectful to the current teaching staff. At the same time, a teacher who is stand-offish can be seen as a push over and not able to contribute. As you know there is a delicate balance for teachers in the classroom and you should be able to get a feel for this during the observation period of the interview.

POST INTERVIEW & HIRING

After the interview, it is imperative to check references as well as anything else you have to check by law (background, criminal history, etc). Listen very carefully while checking references and do not ignore any red flags. Ask references questions specific to your values. It is helpful to ask either/or questions such as "does this person work better alone or on a team" or "if you were to hire this person again, what position would you hire them for."

If you decide not to hire a candidate, contact them and let them know that you have gone another direction. You may or may not want to give them feedback about your decision. Either way it is a professional courtesy to not leave people wondering. If it was positive but not a right fit at the time, you can let them know that you'd like to keep their resume on file if a position opens up. If you decide to hire a candidate extend them an offer to accept or decline. The offer should include a start date, training timeline, and approximate date of their first evaluation. We will talk more about the onboarding process in the next chapter.

ACTION STEPS:

- Take a look around your center to see how the applicants 5 senses will be met.
- Identify your Unique Hiring Benefits or how your unique benefits to parents also benefit your employees.
- Ask your teachers what they want in a team member.
- Collect your favorite behavioral based interview questions on a one-page sheet for your interview.
- Create a check list for your pre, during, and post interview process to make sure everyone who conducts interviews are on the same page.

SUGGESTED READING:

- Read Marcus Buckingham's *Now, Discover your Strengths* or *Strengths Based Leadership*.
- Read Tom Rath's *Strengths Finder 2.0*.

CHAPTER FIVE
ONBOARDING AND TRAINING

WRITTEN OFFER

When you decide to hire a candidate, you should have a training timeline and plan in place before you extend the offer. Start with the date you'd like to have the person full on board in their position and work backwards. Present that timeline with your offer as well as your letter of intent for the potential employee to sign. The letter of intent states that you would both commit to at least one year (or the remainder of the school year) unless there are extenuating circumstances. Although not legally binding because most states are "at will," this letter lets your new employee know that you are committed to the relationship just as much as they are, barring any extenuating circumstances.

CELEBRATE THE HIRE

In the book *Scaling Up*, the author, Verne Harnish, points out the irony that we often have huge celebrations when an individual leaves a company instead of when they are hired. I understand that we often throw parties when people leave to give coworkers and customers an appropriate place to express appreciation and well wishes. It is funny that we don't celebrate a new hire as much, or sometimes at all. All too often, new employees are recognized with an email or by introduction at a staff meeting. Then, we let them fly under the radar as they establish relationships and get the hang of the routine and culture of the school.

Here at Child Care Marketing Solutions we consider the first 90 days the most important when a parent joins the school. The first 90 days of parent retention is the most vital. It is when ambivalent feelings are (or aren't) formed as well as the most pivotal time in relationship building. It is no different with new employees. It is when a new employee will feel the most accepted or isolated in her new position. They will feel like they are appreciated and given information they need OR left alone to figure it out on their own.

PROVIDE STRUCTURE

Having an onboarding and training plan set up in advance can help you make those first 90 days successful. I have an example 90 Day Teacher Retention Plan in Appendix B. As far as training goes, assume no one will read your staff handbook ahead of time. In the event your new employee does read it, she likely won't understand it or be ready to implement it until she actually spends time in her position.

Remember, training is a process and cannot be achieved in one day. When I was a teacher, we had college students working in various capacities (practicum, interns, student teachers, work study, literacy tutors, and so on). Each semester we would hold a 3-hour evening orientation (food provided) to go over the basics. Each week we would meet with the students for a 30 minute "post lab" meeting and break down our policies as well as curriculum into smaller chunks. This was hugely successful for not only the students, but the paid staff in the classroom as well. Each teacher reviewed our policies, procedures, values, and developmentally appropriate classroom practice 2-3 times a year and had to set an example because we were constantly being observed. This provides an opportunity to reassert core values.

Without this common practice, systems will slip away slowly until no one actually knows why they are doing things the way they are. Is it a choice or required? "How do those actions in the room meet core values? I realize this isn't possible in every center due to ratios, classroom coverage, and teacher shifts, but it is important that teachers review your Standard Operating Procedures (SOPs), set an example and hold each other accountable.

TRAINING TECHNIQUES

Again, because I understand meeting for 30 minutes each week with all members on the classroom team may not necessarily be possible, here are three ways to help make your teacher training more of a process. Each one can stand alone or be used in conjunction with the others.

Training Videos

Break your policies (staff manual, policies and procedures, SOPs, or whatever your terminology) down into short videos for your new employee. Short (5-15 mins) videos that show or tell a particular process is an effective way for your new employee to gain buy in and easily understand processes. Video # 1 should be you, the owner, explaining your history and values. Cover why you opened the centers and why they operate the way they do. This video is especially important if you are not onsite or directly involved in the training process.

Teacher Mentor

Have another teacher (not you, the director, or direct supervisor) be responsible for mentoring the new employee. Having someone who isn't the new employee's direct supervisor or employer is important so the new employee feels free to openly ask questions and admit weaknesses. This also gives the new employee another person to get to know and be supported by. That teacher will feel a sense of responsibility to the new employee and your center. She will likely take the new employee under her wing, helping her get to know coworkers as well as your center policies. Owners should request feedback so the mentor is held accountable and to make sure training is done in a timely manner and the mentee feels supported.

Automated "Drip" Policy Emails

Using your CRM or other automated email system (Constant Contact, Mail Chimp, iContact, etc) set up a sequence or a "campaign" of automated emails to be sent out at various times so your new (and current) employees get shorter breakdowns of your policies directly to their inbox. Breaking your handbook and SOPs up into bite size chunks helps your new employees "digest" them more easily. This also allows you to send them in order of importance. The employee will also be able to easily search for them in her inbox. Here is an example:

Subject: Why the heck do we do that?

Hi _____,

I hope things are going well for you so far. You may have looked around and wondered why we do things around here the way we do? Over the next several weeks, I will be sending you emails to help explain. Hopefully these short emails will be quick and simple so that you can figure why the heck we are doing things the way we are!

The first thing I want to explain to you is why we are even open. I talked about it a little during your interview, but read (or click the video) below to find out why I opened Jolly Johnsen's ELC:

[Interesting story or video]

Of course, if you have any questions or suggestions, I am eager to hear!

Ideally you could use all 3 of these ideas by automatically sending your new employees automated videos and having her mentor check in to see if everything is making sense.

EVALUATION:

Your training timeline should include an evaluation around the 60–90 day mark. I prefer 90 days, but it is up to you as long as you make it consistent among employees. At that point, sit down with your new employee for a formal new hire evaluation. You should be able to assess the employee's strengths and areas for growth at this point. This is also a great time to determine if any additional training or professional development would benefit the employee to be successful within your organization.

This process will directly lead into setting goals for the next 9 months, when you would meet again for her 12 month, annual evaluation. Together set goals for the employee which include measureable and time-bound objectives. These goals along with your values should be the basis for evaluation at the 12-month mark and from there on out at each annual evaluation.

Evaluations should be taken seriously. As soon as the employee is hired, put her 60/90-day evaluation on the calendar. At that evaluation, tentatively schedule the next one, and so on. Schedule evaluations on Tuesday, Wednesday, or Thursdays when people are less likely to be out. This will help keep the scheduled date or not require you to have to reschedule as many.

If you are not doing written goals and regular evaluations with your employees, I suggest starting immediately. All employees, no scratch that, all humans work better and have more buy in and motivation when they are working toward one or more goals. Goals give us a purpose and something to achieve and celebrate. Scientifically speaking, each time a goal or objective is met we get a shot of serotonin released in our body that encourages us to keep going. This is our body's way of naturally rewarding us and then motivating us to keep moving forward. Originally, it helped humans survive by hunting and seeking shelter. You can read more about the science in Simon Sinek's *Leaders Eat Last*.

We will cover motivation and buy in even more in the next section of this book, as we address long term employee retention. After you hire and train your employees the goal is to keep them employed at your organization as long as possible. As you learned in the previous chapters, finding, hiring, and training employees is no easy task. The next part of the book is equally, if not more, important so you do not have to repeat the previous process more than necessary.

ACTION STEPS:

- Write out your own staff onboarding plan and check list.
- Evaluate your current training process. What is working? What do you often see staff members forget or has fallen through the cracks?
- Ask your current staff what went well with training and where they were confused. Let existing staff help you create your training plan.
- Create a 90-day evaluation based off of issues that you primarily see with new hires.

SUGGESTED READING:

- Read Vern Harnish *Scaling Up*.

PART TWO
STAFF RETENTION

CHAPTER SIX
LAY THE FOUNDATION FOR KEEPING
GREAT EMPLOYEES

According to industry articles and publications we've seen over the years, after you hire great employees, the next challenge is to keep them. You deserve excellent employees and your children and parents deserve excellent teachers and administration. It's no secret that happy teachers equal happy children, which in turn equal happy parents. If your employees are happy, your clients are happy. Think about in how many companies you actually ever meet the owners, not very many. You interact with the staff at most organizations, and that staff is what you attribute to the reputation of the company.

PROTIP: *Great leaders know that happy teachers equal happy clients and a prosperous program.*

Although we sometimes let ourselves believe it is, money is NOT the number one reason why staff leave. When you hire staff, they know what their pay will be and will not expect it to get exponentially higher. They know what they are signing up for. That is not to say that staff never leave because of money, some find that the field of education is not sustainable, and may leave the industry altogether. If your staff is leaving your organization to go to a similar organization, money is not the only issue they are leaving.

Since our industry makes it difficult to compensate our employees monetarily for the job they do, it's even more important to have great leadership in your program. You've heard the familiar phrase, "people do not leave jobs, they leave managers." That statement is just as true in child care as it is in the corporate world. Don't get me wrong, some of the best decisions I've made are letting unhappy staff walk away and use money as an excuse. But, it is important to recognize that leadership is a big reason staff leave. They leave if they don't feel leadership is capable, responsive, or passionate. Whether or not this is true is, unfortunately, irrelevant. It is the staff's perception. They do not see you lying awake at night praying you can pay them more. They do not see you at your home computer searching for new ideas and cheaper materials so they can have the resources they need.

Industry average annual turnover rate is 35%. If you aren't sure where you stand, take the number of employees you began with this school year and multiply it by .35. This is the number of staff who will likely leave your program this year. So if you started out with 100 employees, you will likely have 35 of them leave within the year. That feels like a lot, and it is. It is comparable with restaurants and retail industries. Part of this is due to wages, yes, but the other challenge is the demographic we hire. We typically hire young women (20-32), who either haven't finished a degreed program or have recently received their BA. Females in this age range are in the most transient age of their lives. They are getting married, having children, and/or finishing educational programs. Because it's impossible not to hire this demographic (they're the majority of your applicants), it is important to hire the right ones and give them reasons to stay.

Before I talk about how to get staff to stay at your program, I want to briefly touch on other reasons why staff leave. Leadership is often a big reason, but the other main reason is other staff members. Even if leadership is great, if you have some negative or underperforming members of the team, your great staff may see them as a huge detriment to the organization. I will talk more in a few chapters about how to determine when it's time for some staff to leave. Other reasons that teachers report leaving is that they don't feel they have opportunities for growth or they aren't challenged.

Over the next several chapters I will outline how to retain teachers in your program. Really think about the reasons I listed before as well as your frustrations in this industry. All too often I hear complaints that as an industry you are seen as baby sitters. Your teachers feel this stigma as well, so it is important that we do not treat them as such. Again, it is about the perception of your staff, not your intentions as a leader.

In Chapter One I emphasized the importance of Values and Trust as the two elements to a great company culture. Those two elements are the driving elements in retaining employees as well. In the book, *The Speed of Trust*, Stephen Covey defines leadership as "getting results in a way that inspires trust." He then breaks down trust as 50% character and 50% competence.

This break down is incredibly important as many people often attribute trust closer to 100% character. Often times, people need more information and sometimes more training to perform the tasks they were hired to perform.

To further explain the composition of trust, Covey gives the example that his father (also Stephen Covey) has excellent character, but he would not trust his father to perform brain surgery. For that particular task, his father would not be competent. This is an extreme example, but illustrates the point well. Many times, we confuse character with competency. In the day to day work of a child care administrator, we often view the lack of competence as a lack of character, and then decide the lack of character is malicious and label our employees as "lazy" or "selfish." While this is sometimes the case, and I will address that in Chapter 12, it often is a really a lack of information, training, or resources.

I like to explain the make-up of Trust with the following acronym Transparency, Relationships, Underlying Values, Systems & Strategy, and Training. In the following chapters I will break down how each of these topics contributes to your program.

ACTION STEPS:

- Calculate your staff retention.
- Identify why staff leave your center, keeping in mind "more pay" might be a generic excuse given.
- Compare the reasons people say they leave to the reasons why your staff said they stay.

SUGGESTED READING:

- Read Stephen Covey's *The Speed of Trust.*

CHAPTER SEVEN
TRANSPARENCY

Overall your culture works best when you have staff buy in. You want your staff to be on board and supporting your overall goal, and/or your reason why. They need to feel connected to the company's core values and operate on behalf of the company. Often time businesses operate on a "need to know" basis. This is a mistake if you want your staff to have buy in. So why does any organization operate this way? Much of this belief is based on fear--- fear that if our employees know how much money we make, they will want to be paid more, fear that someone might be able to do the job we do, fear that we might make a mistake that someone will point out. In fact, the opposite is true. Knowledge is power.

PROTIP:

The more knowledge your employees have about the big picture of your center, the more buy in they will have.

The more information people have, the more likely they will work towards the big picture. If employees don't know or understand the overall goal, they will feel disconnected and not included. As a result, they will likely lack the motivation to carry out tasks that seemingly have no meaning to them. Bottom line: employees need to know why they are doing what they are asked to do. Hopefully they will understand and achieve buy in. The four main areas in your program that should be transparent are expectations, calendars, enrollment, and budget.

EXPECTATIONS

Expectations should be clear, stated, and inspected. Do not assume that people know what to do or that they will actually do it. While I assume it is common sense to smile and introduce myself to a parent walking in the classroom, it may feel uncomfortable to a teacher. She or he may think they are supposed to act like one would if the parent wasn't in the room, to see the room "in action." It is important to include these expectations in your staff training. Too often we hold a staff meeting about these topics, and then they get lost or disoriented as old staff leave and new people are hired. As one of our clients, Paul Huff says, "What gets inspected, gets respected." So make sure you have a system to make sure these practices are in place the way you have set the expectations. It may seem backwards, but the more you let staff know your expectations, the less questions they will come to you with. If your staff know what your overall goal is, they will have more autonomy and feel confident making decisions for themselves.

Here are the common instances in which we should set clear expectations with teachers:

Answering the Phone

Expectations should be set for both administration and classroom teachers because many of you have your phones routed to the classroom if no one answers in the office. When this happens, we not only add another stressor to the teacher's environment, we also expect them to handle the phone call with ease as if they were in a quiet place. Both teacher and administrators should have a script on how to answer the phone. If you get push backs about having a script, give your employees simple guidelines on what information to collect on the phone call.

The goal of any phone call from a new parent is to schedule a tour. Do you want your classroom teachers to aim for this goal? Or would you rather them get the parents information for your director to call back? What should they say if the parent asks them about prices? Have your teachers practice answering the phone in a chaotic classroom. Let them know what to say if the director is not present. I can't tell you how many times I've heard "No, the director isn't here that much, she usually leaves at noon." Even if that is the case, that response gives the impression that the program is left unsupervised. "Our director isn't available right now, but I know she'd love to tell you about the program, can I get your number and she will call you back. It might be tomorrow morning before she gets a chance, is that ok?" Lastly, give your teachers permission to let the phone call go to voicemail if there is a lot of background noise, commotion, or if answering the phone would be to the detriment of a child. They shouldn't always let it go to voicemail, but I can tell you from experience, hearing a stressed out teacher or screaming child is not the first impression you want to give a potential new parent.

Greeting Parents

Let staff know it is an expectation that they smile and say hello to parents at the center. This includes all parents at all places in the center, whether it be in the classroom or in the hallways. The reason behind this is to create a warm environment where everyone feels welcome.

Many people are unaware of their resting face and have to make a genuine effort to smile at people, otherwise they tend to look angry. It's a common problem, but not everyone is aware of the problem and need to be taught to understand these hidden messages. Let your staff know if they need to consciously make eye contact and smile to avoid looking angry or unhappy.

Let your teachers know how they should behave if the director brings a tour through their classroom. Often, staff and teachers feel that the tour should be authentic and a view of the program "in action." They act as if the tour is not happening and try to go on as normal. The truth is, that is awkward and creates an unfriendly feeling. Everyone should greet parents on the tour and introduce themselves. Each person can talk about what they are doing and offer an explanation instead of letting the parents figure it out through observation.

PROTIP: *Everyone should greet parents on the tour and introduce themselves.*

Let staff know the perceptions of their behavior in the classroom. All staff should know the expectations on exactly what they should be doing during working hours. They should be told how to behave in the classroom, on the playground, and during field trips. Set up the expectation on the specific verbiage and tone teachers should use if there is a behavioral issue on a field trip. This may feel like it would fall under your policies and procedures. In fact, work conduct is much more than that.

I remember I once had to bring a child back from a walking field trip because he was hurting his friends. As I struggled to carry the screaming child back, I felt like I was making a huge scene and drawing lots of negative attention to the situation. Instead of walking with my head down getting the child back as quickly as possible, I kept repeating, *"I am so sorry, [child's name], I wish we could have stayed at the plaza too, next time we will keep our hands and feet to ourselves"* in a very calm and soothing manner. The child then started screaming "I won't kick my friends anymore" giving any onlookers a fuller story of what was going on. I actually had people approach me offering to help and telling me they had to deal with the same thing with their own children.

Participating in Social Media

We suggest you check with your lawyers, but you should have a policy on social media. Most states do not allow you to make policies restricting your employees and parents "friending" on social media. Also, you cannot force your staff to become your friends, although I do suggest you try and friend your employees. Because laws regulate what you can mandate on social media, educated staff is vital when it comes to this sensitive issue.

Educate staff on social media presence and how much it can affect a parent's view of them and the school. Also, on Social Media such as Facebook, parents can view who is online and when things are posted. The time of postings could cause a lot of insecurity if parents are seeing posts throughout the day when they think the teacher should be with the children.

You can also send a friendly reminder to parents that as a professional courtesy to your teachers, you don't encourage social media relationships to protect your staff's privacy when not at work

Again, check with your lawyer to see what your state law and best practice is around Social Media. Unfortunately, there is often not a lot you can do besides trust that your staff and parents will make good decisions on social media. If you're hiring the right people, this should not be a big concern.

Teacher/Family Interaction in Public

You cannot control how your staff acts outside of their working hours, but you can set up the expectation of what behavior is permitted while on the school property. I once had a staff member that thought as soon as she clocked out, she was free to do whatever she wanted. Her outer sweater came off, leaving her in a strapless tank top, exposing a multitude of tattoos and skin, clearly violating the dress code. I had to explain to her that as long as she was on the school property the dress code would to be enforced.

You may also want to educate staff on what to do if they see parents and children outside of the workplace. Again, you can't control this, but you can set up an expectation that you would prefer the teachers follow. Many might not know how to act if they see parents and children outside the school. If you have hired the right people, this won't be an issue and you can trust it will not cause you any problems. However, families sometimes cross boundaries, especially in public asking questions or taking the teacher's time. You can coach your staff to be willing to talk to parents, but if they feel uncomfortable to politely say, "will you send me an email and let's talk more about that subject on Monday."

Parent Emails and Phone Calls

Believe it or not, on several occasions I've seen staff give out their personal email and phone numbers to parents to try and be helpful. Your staff should have access to an email account (hopefully one to themselves) and a phone number that they can use to communicate with parents. Let staff know what topics are appropriate for emails and phone calls. You certainly don't want your teachers emailing parents letting them know their child had a bad day, that would be an appropriate face to face or phone conversation. Let staff know how to respond if a parent is trying to communicate about sensitive issues via email or text as well. Give them key phrases or words to use if a parent does start this communication. Let them know they are welcome to copy or blind copy you or the director for support.

CALENDARS

I highly recommend using shared calendars. This is important for two reasons. First, you want to keep everyone apprised of deadlines and events. The second reason is so everyone knows what each other is doing. This helps eliminate interruptions as well as misinterpretations. We often coach our clients to schedule one on one time with staff weekly, bi-weekly, or monthly. This gives staff scheduled time in the office with the director. This gives them a scheduled forum for support or any concerns. We have seen this cut down on gossip, questions are getting answered, and any miscommunications where your staff feel like they don't get the information they need first hand is solved.

Many of the tasks that owners and directors do are behind the scenes or can be done off site. All too often, this conveys the feeling that nothing is actually being done by administrators. If your employees do not see that management is also putting in equal effort, they may feel resentful. This happens more often around the end of the semester when burn out is likely to occur. Everyone starts evaluating what others are doing. It's human nature to look around when you start to feel exhausted and see who isn't holding up their end of the bargain. If the expectation is set that everyone is pulling their weight and happy to show it on the calendar, this resentment will happen less and less.

The calendar is also a great place to model balance. If you record your vacations and personal appointments, it will encourage your staff to do the same. Taking planned time off for vacation and personal appointments is much better than calling in sick once life takes its toll and gives unplanned vacations. This reinforces honesty and value placed on life balance.

PROTIP: *Teachers should calculate the Full Time Equivalency for their classroom each month.*

ENROLLMENT

Aside from making cubbies and taking attendance, teachers are often left out of the enrollment process. Unfortunately, we are all sadly disappointed when said teacher or staff member sighs or rolls their eyes at yet another new student. Especially if you have a lot of part time students, the new child is often seen as more work for the teacher and isn't exactly greeted with open arms. Here is information you should share with staff and teachers as far as enrollment:

Classroom Full Time Equivalency (FTE)

How many children does it take for your school to actually be full? Many people think "my classroom holds 24 students, and I have 30, I MUST be full." Teachers may not be aware that sometimes it takes 2, 3 or even 4 children to fill one spot or one FTE. Have each teacher be in charge of tracking the FTE in their own classroom and knowing how many more children it will take to have a full room. This will change their mindset and encourage them to help the room get and stay full.

School FTE

Keep track of where you are as school FTEs in a public area at the center so teachers know which classrooms need more children. They may know people or have great ideas on how to monetize the space better (i.e. if children could be ready to move classrooms earlier or stay longer).

Classroom Break Even Analysis

Each staff member should have a good idea on each classroom's breakeven point. This means how many students does it take to cover pay for the teachers and resources in the room. If they understand that infants are often loss leaders (basically rooms that feed into the other rooms and attract multi-children families), they will understand why the other rooms need to have more children to make up for losses elsewhere. It will also help them understand why you keep them working at ratio instead of having extra adults in the classroom.

Withdrawals

Your staff should also know what a withdrawal costs the center. This gives them the big picture on why relationships with children and families are so important. Of course the most important reason is always the well-being of the child, but from a business standpoint, these relationships have a big impact as well. It is always easier to maintain an existing client than the costs needed to attract a new one.

BUDGET

In most centers I have worked with, the budget is not common knowledge shared with teachers. Many people keep their budget a secret on purpose, because it is complicated and never really "complete." Other schools have just not thought to share it with staff because the staff is not directly affected by the numbers.

If your staff knows your rates and is able to do basic math, they likely know how much money is coming into your center. If they don't know where the money is actually going, they will assume it's merely lining your pockets. This creates a problem if your staff already feels underpaid, which they likely do. I'm not suggesting you publish your Profit and Loss Statement, but it is helpful to give staff a routine breakdown on your expenditures.

PROTIP: *Give staff an annual break down of expenditures, so they have an idea where tuition goes.*

It can be as simple as the pie chart shown on the following page. You don't have to give exact numbers or figures, just let them know how much it costs on average to run the center. Many of them have no clue how much your mortgage or insurance costs you. This has been a game changer for people whose staff feel highly underpaid or taken advantage of. If they

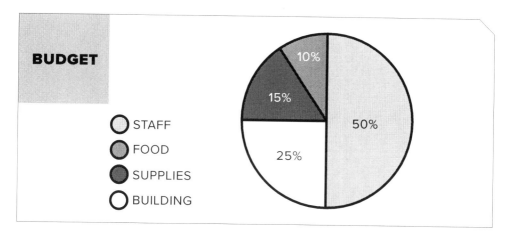

see administration (or even other teachers) driving fancy cars or wearing designer apparel, they will feel their efforts are going towards someone else's lavish lifestyle.

The other unknown expense is often supplies. Many times, staff who feel like they don't have the resources they need, think that you may be skimping on supplies. Attaching figures and percentages to these numbers let your teachers know what is going on with the income coming into school. Staff may start to utilize supply closets better or become creative with existing supplies. You never want teachers to spend their own money on supplies. Let them know how you utilize the budget, and let them have a say in what supplies are in their classrooms.

PROTIP: *Let teachers have a say in what supplies they would like in their classroom and a process for getting last minute supplies.*

Another great idea that one of our clients, Arianne Betazzi from California, is implementing is line itemizing all of the staff's benefits and bonuses. This helps staff see how much your organization is actually spending on them. They may only make nine dollars an hour, but when you figure in health and any other benefits you have, they are actually getting a lot more than they think. This helps give your staff an overall appreciation of what they mean to you as an employee.

Transparency is vital to running a successful business and keeps everyone working towards the same goals. Another area of transparency that is worth mentioning if you have a staff guilty of gossiping, is open-door meetings. If the owner or director's door is always shut during meetings, it causes angst amongst staff. The human mind automatically assumes there are secrets and negativity if information is being hidden. Caution: do not adopt an "open-door" policy if you do not plan to use it ALL of the time. That will cause even more upheaval if the door closes at a point in time. If you do have an open-door policy and need to have a semi-private meeting, it is best done off-site. Again, the idea is to have everyone on the same road towards the same goal. Try to include everyone in big picture details that are important to accomplish this goal. The next layer of trust that is equally important is Relationships.

ACTION STEPS:

- List any expectations that are not being met by all employees at your program.
- Identify areas where you need to further explain or document expectations. At your next staff meeting clarify those expectations.
- Make sure your staff handbook covers all of the areas you identified.
- Create a document that helps staff understand what Full Time Equivalency (FTE) is and how it is calculated in each classroom.
- Create an overview of your budget breakdown with percentages. Share it with your staff.

CHAPTER EIGHT
RELATIONSHIPS

Relationships are a fundamental part of life. They are as important professionally as they are personally. However, the boundaries are often more confusing in a professional environment. Balancing professional relationships with and between employees can be a challenge. You really want your employees to be friends so they enjoy coming to work and working as a team. On the flip side, you want to make sure they act professional at work and that other employees don't feel left out if people talk about non-work related outings. As a leader, it is a challenge to be friendly with employees but still be in the leadership role. We highly suggest having monthly outings with staff as team building, but making sure that you still maintain professional conversation topics and boundaries.

My favorite analogy when talking about relationships is the piggy bank. This is often how I taught my students to relate to children as well. Think about the deposits and credits you put into everyone's bank account. Often when we hire an employee we immediately start placing demands on them and taking credits out of their "bank account." I understand that this is part of the employee-employer relationship. This is why building positive bonds with employees right away and encouraging positive relationships with coworkers are essential.

The biggest challenge is that deposits in a person's bank account must be intended AND received as *genuine* deposits. People often tell you to always "give three positives to one negative." Unless this is done carefully, it is automatically seen as inauthentic. If someone sits down with me to talk about something and starts listing off three generic compliments, I will not take those to heart and will immediately anticipate impending negative or constructive criticism. I don't see those positives as genuine, I view them as a disguise to tell me the bad news. The point is that you need to be building your positive bank account with people when there is nothing negative to say. Take time to cultivate a relationship when there isn't an evaluation of a task or project.

<table>
<tr><td>**PRO**TIP:</td><td>*If you build a positive relationship with staff in the beginning they will have more buy in when things get challenging around the center. Your staff must feel personally connected to his or her team.*</td></tr>
</table>

One way to help cultivate relationships between staff members is by having them take personality assessments. The more people know about each other, the more they understand each other. The more they understand about each other, the less they view each other's actions as personal. Personal assessments create an awareness and sensitivity about how to treat each other. If I understand that my coworker is introverted and avoids confrontation, I will view her less as passive aggressive and be certain to choose words more carefully if I have an issue. If my coworkers know that I am outgoing and handle conflict directly, they will hopefully view me as less aggressive. There are a multitude of personality assessments out there including Enneagram, Myers Briggs, Myers Briggs Conflict, HumanMetrics, The Big 5 Personality, Personality Colors, and so on. There are personality assessments, leadership assessments, conflict assessments, and so on. Myers–Briggs assessment are the most widely used.

No matter which you use, the key is to have everyone take the same test(s) and then USE the information. I have taken a million of these assessments for my sorority and for employers and we all just walk away knowing a little more about ourselves or the people at our table. We rarely use them after that, possibly referring to them one or two times in the future, when we have new people who we promise to have take the test as well. Knowing information about yourself is powerful, but the key to these assessments being meaningful in your work environment is making them common language for all. Post the results for each classroom team. Email out a matrix of where everyone falls. The benefit to these assessments is there is no "right" or "wrong" way to be, it is what it is. Hopefully everyone is a little different and unique.

This leads to me to the Strengths Finder Assessment which was brought up in the hiring section of the book. The Strengths Finder concept which identifies natural strengths was cultivated by Marcus Buckingham in his book, *Now, Discover Your Strengths*. Buckingham's main point is that if we are working within our strengths, our work should come naturally to us and be more enjoyable. It is more fun to expand on our strengths and develop them than to be "well rounded" and try and develop our weaknesses. Instead, run "damage control" on weaknesses i.e. develop them enough so they aren't costly to your work environment. Management should hire people with enough different strengths that they have well rounded teams.

Buckingham recognizes 34 strengths broken into four categories:

EXECUTING
- Achiever
- Arranger
- Belief
- Consistency
- Deliberative
- Discipline
- Focus
- Responsibility
- Restorative

INFLUENCING
- Activator
- Command
- Communication
- Competition
- Maximizer
- Self-Assurance
- Significance
- WOO

STRATEGIC
- Analytical
- Context
- Futuristic
- Ideation
- Input
- Intellection
- Learner
- Strategic

RELATIONSHIP BUILDING
- Adaptability
- Connectedness
- Developer
- Empathy
- Harmony
- Includer
- Individualization
- Positivity
- Relator

According to Buckingham, if leaders focus on their employee's strengths, 75% of employees will become engaged in their work, compared to 9% when strengths are not a focus by management. The book suggests that you focus on a person's top 5 strengths. Once you have everyone's strengths, list them in a matrix. I have put an example matrix below.

	Executing	Influencing	Relationship-Building	Strategic
Person 1	Achiever	Maximizer (1) Activator (2) Significance	Positivity	
Person 2		Woo (2) Maximizer Communication	Positivity (1)	Input
Person 3	Achiever (1) Responsibility (2) Discipline		Relator	Learner
Person 4	Achiever (1)	Maximizer	Relator	Futuristic (2) Strategic
Person 5		Maximizer	Harmony (2) Relator	Learner (1) Intellection
Next Person We Hire:		Secondary	Primary	

Assessments should be used by management to relate to staff members as well. In the book *StrengthsFinder 2.0* by Tom Rath, there is a breakdown of all of the strengths and the characteristics of people who display them. We sometimes have two staff members come to the front of the room (usually who are a teaching team) and read about their strengths out loud. It's like a light bulb goes off in the room. *"Oh she does do that. That makes so much sense."* The book *Strengths Based Leadership* by Tom Rath talks about how to lead people of different strengths. If you are having an issue with a particular

PROTIP: *Conduct a genuine team building activity at each staff meeting.*

staff member it may be worth it to look up how to relate to that person.
    If you are having a hard time with your staff relating to you or each other, here are some team building activities that you can start incorporating

at your staff meetings. Note - while I do think some sort of lesson or team building is important at each staff meeting, make sure that they are different enough that staff doesn't start to dread the team building time or giving answers just to get through it.

1. In the book The 5 Dysfunctions of a team. The first dysfunction is lack of trust. The book offers the following three questions to build trust among employees. The purpose is to acquire a personal understanding of your co-workers and why they think the way they do. Here are the questions:
    a. Where did you grow up?
    b. How many kids are in your family?
    c. What was the most difficult or important challenge of your childhood?
2. Penny Game - Pass around a jar of pennies, have everyone grab a penny. Each person looks at the date on the penny, and tells something that happened in their life during that year. You may need to choose pennies ahead of time so they are appropriate years for your staff ages.
3. Things People May Not Know - Each staff member writes something people don't know about them on a sticky note. All sticky notes go into a pile. Designate someone to read off each note. The remaining players try and guess who the note belongs to.
4. Strengths Finder - Have each team member take the Strengths Finder and share their strengths with the rest of the team.
5. Myers Briggs - have each team member take the Myers Briggs assessment and discuss the findings with a team.
6. Myers Briggs Conflict - Have each team member take the conflict assessment. This one is really great for encouraging productive conflict around the office. If you know that some people are more forward with their conflict, confrontations will seem less aggressive. If people shy away from conflict, they won't seem as dismissive.
7. Bring a favorite childhood toy - If people are from out of state, they may have to settle with bringing a picture. Have each member explain what the toy meant to him or her.
8. Favorite Childhood Book - and what it meant to them when they read it as a child.
9. Favorite Childhood Movie - what they liked about it.

10. 10 Things they have in Common - have team members pair up or get into small groups and find ten things they have common.
11. Draw a favorite memory from a child and then share their drawing.
12. First Job/Worst Job - Have each team member share their first or worst job.
13. One Word Descriptions - these are good for in between meetings so that team building doesn't get to be too common. Have staff go around and describe what the words means to them. Examples of words:
    a. Team
    b. Conflict
    c. Teamwork
    d. Productivity
    e. Education
    f. Learning
    g. Play
    h. Assessment

There are countless other activities that you can find online. The goal is to help team members know each other, find some commonalities and become supportive. This foundation will be helpful when everyone starts to feel burnt out, they know each other well enough to not get snippy with each other, or even worse, the children or parents.

ACTION STEPS:

- List any personality or strengths assessments you have taken. Which did you like and why?
- Research with assessments would best fit your organization.
- Have your staff take assessments on their own or together. Make sure to review results as a group and have a document showing everyone's results.

SUGGESTED READING:

- *Now Discover Your Strengths*, Marcus Buckingham
- *Strengths Based Leadership*, Tom Rath
- *Strengths Finder 2.0*, Tom Rath
- *5 Dysfunctions of a Team*, Patrick Lencioni

CHAPTER NINE
UNDERLYING VALUES

We discussed values at length in chapter one. The good thing about values is that they set you and your team up for success from day one. Just like at Southwest, if your values dictate your underlying culture, this culture will shine through to the children and families you serve at your school. Oftentimes, your values skip over your staff and address your clients. While this is understandable, it is also a way to set yourself for failure. Yes, you want to serve your clients, but your values should dictate how you serve your clients. If you want staff buy in and to actually utilize the values, then they must be a part of what you value.

PROTIP: *Your values should dictate how and why you serve your clients*

As I mentioned before, here at Child Care Marketing Solutions, we value fun and optimism. Because I know that these are two of our values, I know that I can joke around with our clients and build personal relationships with them. We are not a stuffy company that is "by the book." We host cocktail parties at our meetings and have dinner with clients when we are onsite.

Another example I will give is progressive. When schools are progressive, they are open to ideas and moving forward. They have a system for employees to give suggestions and new ideas. They don't jump on every idea, but they give their staff the opportunity to add to the school.

One challenge you may have with values is that they can undermine all of your staff management efforts IF leaders are not living and breathing by their values 110%. Here is the other kicker – it's not about whether you think you are living your values. It's about your staff's perception. Do you say you value teamwork, but then make all major decisions alone, or just with senior management? Is one of your values Customer First or Families First, but you talk negatively about parents? Do you claim to value integrity but allow employees to gossip?

PROTIP: *Leaders should live and breathe your values 110%.*

All of these things can erode trust and unfortunately trust is not isolated per value. If you aren't displaying one value, likely the rest go by the wayside as well. I would say the biggest misconception of your values is where enrollment is concerned. Do your teachers see how a full school fits into your values? If you value education and one on one interaction, a full school might not seem in alignment with your values. If you talk about making more money because of those enrollments, it probably REALLY doesn't seem in alignment with your values. I'm not suggesting not to be full or talk about revenue with your staff. Instead, make sure employees understand how enrollment and, in turn, revenue, fit into your values and vision. This might require some soul searching on your end.

If revenue and your values seem unrelated, you're missing the mark, especially if you're constantly talking about enrollment. Why? Because that will then replace your values as the goal. It replaces your "why." If your staff think that you care more about revenue than your values, your values have essentially gone out the window.

Luckily this one is a simple fix. You can have a conversation with your staff about what it means to be full and how that positively impacts your values (tie it together) and then change your language. You do not want enrollments solely to generate revenue. You want to positively impact more children's lives.... yes, it takes money to do that, and everyone should be compensated, but the child is the value.

Use your values as your common language at your schools. Bring them up in casual conversation and make decisions based off them. Then, you will lead by example to your staff on what you're trying to accomplish. Hold your staff accountable for living by your values. Ask them to tell stories about how they made decisions based off of your core values.

You want to make sure you have a system in place to help you reward and appreciate your team for living by your values. Many people have heard of the *5 Love Languages* by Gary Chapman. He also has written *The 5 Languages of Appreciation in the Work Place.* In this book, Chapman recognizes that not all people like to be appreciated in the same way. While some employees would like to stand up in front of a crowd and have you thank them publicly, that could be a nightmare to other employees. The 5 Languages of Appreciation are:

1. Words of Affirmation
2. Quality Time
3. Acts of Service
4. Tangible Gifts
5. Physical Touch

You may already have a good guess about which employees like to be appreciated which way. If not, have them take the assessment. It's important that you are able to show appreciation in a way your employees will actually receive.

PROTIP: *Know how each individual person likes to be appreciated and motivated.*

It is important to understand the difference between appreciation and motivation. Showing appreciation can often motivate your staff to keep up the good work, but that is not always the case. Appreciation is showing someone you noticed what already happened and you are thankful for it. Motivation is inspiring someone to take action or behave a certain way. Your people will naturally be motivated when they have true buy in to your values. However, motivation is a feeling that comes and goes, and you have to find out what motivates some people over others.

Take notes about when your staff gets excited. Is it when they have healthy competition? Is it when they learn new skills or get new resources? Are they motivated by extrinsic rewards when a certain goal is met? Every person has a combination of internal and external factors that motivate them. You can learn more about how people are individually motivated by reading the book "What Motivates Me" by Adrian Gostick and Chester Elton.

ACTION STEPS:

- Make sure your Core Values are defined and you use them as common language. List ways that you could utilize them more at your center.
- Identify ways you can get your staff more involved in exhibiting core values and using them in decision making.
- Have your staff take the Languages of Appreciation quiz to find out how they are best appreciated.
- Note what gets your staff members most excited. Try and personalize motivation techniques based off of this information.

SUGGEST READING:

- *5 Languages of Appreciation in the Work Place*, Gary Chapman
- *All In: How the Best Managers Create a Culture of Belief and Drive Big Results*, Adrian Gostick, Chester Elton

CHAPTER TEN
SYSTEMS AND STRATEGY

Systems and strategy is the next area that helps you build trust within your employees. It is important for your center to be predictable in your practices and processes. Employees should be aware of strategies that meet adopted goals. While this does include day to day operation, your operations manual would be a whole book in itself to go through. The three areas in Systems and Strategy that are the focus within the industry are Evaluation, Accountability, and Delegation.

> **PRO**TIP: *Use the online tool SurveyMonkey to complete anonymous surveys.*

EVALUATION

There are 4 types of evaluations you should be conducting at your center each year:

Parent Surveys of the Center

We recommend using Survey Monkey for online surveys, but no matter what you use, it is important to survey your parents each year and at the same time of year. We recommend doing parents surveys either at the end of the year or before you start registering for the upcoming school year. This is when rate increases naturally occur and you want a chance to fix any underlying issues parents are having, or a plan to fix them, before raising rates so you don't lose any families. This survey is also a great time to re-evaluate any subscriptions or purchases you've made at your center.

Send a thank you and broad overview of the results to your parents and staff. You don't have to tell them how many people responded or what the exact responses were, just what in general everyone is happy about and actions you are going to take going forward to address anything that was stated as a concern. This email shows appreciation to parents who did take the time to fill out the survey, and it lets the other parents know that you do take action based off of the survey results.

> **PRO**TIP: *Follow up with staff and parents letting them know the broad overview of survey results.*

Staff Surveys

Similarly, send out a staff survey to get a program-wide idea for how your staff feel things are going. Anonymous surveys are a great way to get honest feedback from your staff. Ask your staff what they would do differently if they were the director. Ask them what they like best about working at your program, and of course, what they like least. Staff surveys are a great way to give your staff members a voice, and to stay on top of any other issues that may be going on at your center. The other thing that is really great about staff surveys is that you can put numbers on how many staff feel a certain way. Instead of saying "most of the staff hates our snack menu," you can say "five staff members, or 20% feel we can improve our snack menu."

Send an overview of your results to the staff for many of the same reasons that you want to send an overview to the parents. You want your staff to know you heard what they had to say and that it was a good use of their time. You also want to let staff who did not take the time to fill out the survey know that they may have lost their "vote" so to speak on what could be changed at the program.

Self-Evaluation

All staff at the center, including management and owners, should conduct a self-evaluation. You will get just as much or more from self-reflection as you will from peer or supervisor evaluations. Remember, we tend to judge ourselves by our intentions and others by their actions. The intent is to ensure each person reviews their own actions and makes goals to align them with their intentions. We are definitely our own hardest critics. A self-evaluation is also a great way to see if your employees are engaged. Your employees who really take the time to evaluate themselves are probably you're "A" employees who want to improve their skills and learn more.

Employee Evaluation

This can include 360 Peer Reviews, which are reviews done by coworkers and management as well as the supervisor or solely an employee evaluation done by the direct supervisor. Personally, I suggest doing 360 reviews for administration and evaluations for staff. As mentioned in chapter 5, evaluations should include written goals, training needed, and opportunities for growth. Evaluations should be done at least annually and employee goals should be looked at every 90 days.

ACCOUNTABILITY

In the book The "5 Dysfunctions of a Team" by Patrick Linscioni, dysfunction number 4 is avoidance of accountability. You want to make sure staff is held accountable for their actions. Not holding staff accountable may create a slippery slope where other staff members might see what they can 'get away with because so and so did.' The trick here is to approach staff with trust and respect. Instead of asking why they did what they did or didn't do, ask them how you can support them to meet the goal next time. By approaching your staff members with respect, you are giving them the chance to correct the behavior without feeling defensive. You are also letting them know that you notice when they are not meeting expectations.

Although accountability as a word often feels negative, accountability is actually an extremely positive thing. That is because the perception is that staff is held accountable only when they miss the mark on something. While this may feel true, you should be celebrating those who hit the mark as well. You should assign responsibility and check in with staff to make sure that things are running smoothly, and if they run into any problems, you can help them trouble shoot. If you are holding staff accountable, you are celebrating when they hit milestones and openly discussing any issues. Furthermore, if staff who do meet expectations are getting the same bonuses and rewards as staff who do not meet those same expectations, you are sending a message that you do not care who hits or misses.

PROTIP: *Make Accountability a positive aspect by rewarding those who meet expectations and helping those who don't.*

Again, it is important to clearly state your expectation. Instead of saying "no clumping on the playground" it is important to lay out your reasoning and expectation. *"I know the playground is a place for the children to engage with each other while getting fresh air and large motor exercise. And while, we want the children to have freedom from too much instruction on the playground, we still want active learning to be taking place. Many accidents happen on the playground (scraped knees, bumped heads, etc), while these may not be preventable, it might leave parents feeling like the children aren't as supervised. I'd like to see at least two organized activities (obstacle courses, hop scotch, outside art) going on during outside time."* Then reward those teaches who organize activities as well as let the whole staff know when accidents go down on the playground.

Another way to help staff meet expectations and be accountable is through incentive programs. Many of your staff members are millennials and grew up as part of the "sticker generation," myself included. We got a sticker for turning in a paper and a trophy for showing up. Do I think that's right or fair? Doesn't matter, it happened. (For the record, I'm not personally behind that philosophy, but it STILL doesn't matter.) We were "positively rewarded" or "incentivized" for doing what we should be doing anyway. It's really extrinsic motivation and we all see it and do it every day. Disclaimer: this is a generalization and not true of ALL millennials. If you are or know millennials who do not need to be incentivized, that is wonderful too.

This is why incentive programs are becoming so popular. I often get the question "why should we reward people for doing what they should do in the first place?" I couldn't agree more, when you hire someone to do a job, they should do that job for the agreed upon price. However, after we hire someone all of the "and other duties as apply" section of the job description often becomes bigger than the actual job description. Now especially if you are working with millennials who have already been classically conditioned to expect a reward for doing what we should do, those are the things that start to build resentment and de-motivation.

Incentive programs are often the happy medium for management to reward employees for those extra tasks that their job description technically does not include. They also motivate staff to do those things with a smile on their face. If you have the right people in place you will want to incentivize them and give them extra rewards whenever possible. On the reverse, if you have employees that you hate incentivizing or rewarding, it might be time to rethink employment. However, if not planned out effectively they can have adverse effects on your outcome as well as culture. There are a couple guidelines to follow when designing your incentive program:

First – Be clear that no one will be penalized for not participating. Incentives should reward those for going above and beyond. For those employees who are content with their salary and want to focus on the core tasks for which they were hired, no incentive system is required. Set clear expectations.

Second – Let your employees know the reason why you are offering incentives for what you want them to do. I.E. if they participate on the tour, and the tour enrolls, they get a percentage of registration. The rationale is you are doing this because teacher participation helps get the parent to enroll.

Third – Make sure it doesn't encourage competition at the expense of valued team work. In my opinion, there is nothing wrong with a little healthy competition. However, be cautious that everyone has the chance to earn the same incentives for the same tasks.

Incentive programs have been widely adopted and are successful in many organizations, including child care. They can be a great motivator as well as a way of showing appreciation for those workers who routinely go above and beyond in their work. Many of our clients only give incentives if day to day expectations such as arriving on time and keeping the classroom tidy, are met.

The last thing I want to mention as far as accountability goes, is program accountability. I recommend keeping a "dashboard" or "score card" goals that the center is working towards. In a public place, track phone calls, enrollments, withdrawals, and any other metric you are measuring. This way all staff know where the organization stands in reaching its goals. If we lose sight of where we are in the process of working towards a goal, we will likely lose sight of the goal. Encourage your staff members to keep their own personal score card or check list of their own goals as well.

PROTIP:	*Let your employees know the "score" by keeping relevant information such as enrollment, FTEs, and withdrawals in a public place.*

DELEGATION

Instead of "delegation" I prefer to use the word "entrust," although "delegation" is more widely recognized for this discussion. However, to entrust captures what I actually want you to do. Delegation should be part of your normal systems and strategies at your program. Not only does it make management less of a bottle neck, it can give other employees a sense of pride, accomplishment and belonging, if the jobs are done correctly. Make sure you are trusting your employees to do a great job. You are giving them enough guidance to do a great job, but not too much that they feel micro-managed. Staff who have autonomy at work are more likely to report being happy with their work environment, according to the book "All In," by Adrian Gostick and Chester Elton.

Here are the 6 keys to successful delegation:

    1. Ask who is willing to do a task/project for you. Having a volunteer will immediately help you reduce the tension of adding to someone's work load. Maybe the person you

think would be best for the job has personal reasons not to volunteer such as extra stress at home. In this case, the timing would be off. This is a really great way to find new skills among your employees.

PROTIP: *Give specific details when delegating so your staff know exactly what they are being asked to do.*

2. Specify what, why, & how. Communicate exactly what you need. Avoid saying things like, "I need some help with the upcoming open house." Instead, give more specific directions. " I have to pick up the cakes at 4 p.m. on Friday, so I need some help with setting up tables, decorating the 4-year-old room, and laying out brochures for the open house on Friday evening. We usually have less children after 3 p.m. so you can combine classrooms if you need."

3. The why and the how are for bigger projects where you potentially need buy in. For example, "I need someone to document all morning responsibilities as we update our handbook. This way we can have new staff read the staff handbook and will be more prepared to be helpful upon their start date."

4. Give a deadline. This way he or she knows the urgency and when their part will be completed. Create a timeline for big projects and share it with everyone. It is important to follow through on your part. That is, if someone completed their part for the project by the requisite time, and then management does not look at it for several weeks, is frustrating to the person who worked hard to meet the original deadline.

PRO**TIP:** *Trust your employees to do what you have asked them to do. Do not redo their work.*

5. Trust that you have hired competent people who can handle tasks. Let people surprise you. Everyone does things differently and as long as they get finished, that is all that matters. Avoid re-doing someone's work if at all possible. That will de-motivate your staff and discourage them from volunteering again.

6. Give appreciation and credit. Be sure to thank and recognize those employees who go out of their way to be helpful. It seems so simple, but often a "Thank You" can go a long way. Most importantly, give credit to those employees who help you.

The final part of successful delegation is knowing the difference between Accountability vs. Responsibility vs. Authority. While many people may be responsible for getting a project done, only one person can be accountable to make sure the project gets done. If more than one person is accountable, then no one is accountable. The person who is accountable for making sure the project is done may not have the authority to do anything about employees who don't do their part. Here is an example. Mary owns the company and wants her director, Sally, to make sure the staff handbook gets written. Sally entrusts Bill, Susan, and Mike to help her write the handbook. Billy, Susan, and Mike are responsible for doing their parts. Sally is accountable that the handbook gets done and Mary has authority to approve the handbook and get it printed.

These systems and strategies should be used over and over again so that the processes at your center become predictable. Staff knows what to expect and they know their work will get rewarded. This helps with consistency as well as opportunity for them to excel in their work environment and keeps staff motivation high. As one of our clients, Carol Gatewood, would say, if something isn't working at your center, first look at your systems in place, 95% of the time there is a policy or training issue. Make sure you are giving your staff the competency to perform their job tasks and hopefully you won't see as many character issues. This leads us into the final aspect of the TRUST model, training.

ACTION STEPS:

- Plan when you will conduct your annual parent and staff surveys.
- Plan when you will conduct your annual staff evaluations.
- Write down areas where your staff aren't being held accountable.
- Identify specific areas where you would like staff members to go above and beyond. Can you reward those who are currently going above and beyond?
- Would an incentive plan help others be motivated to go above and beyond?
- Write down tasks that you currently do that you can delegate to others.

SUGGESTED READING:

- Read *What Motivates Me*, by Adrian Gostick and Chester Elton

CHAPTER ELEVEN
TRAINING

The final aspect in our TRUST model for employee retention is training. Are you giving your staff the information, resources, and training they need? Keep in mind that no one wakes up and thinks *"What can I do to be mediocre today?"* While I definitely see people who are unsatisfied with their job clock in and out without caring, I still don't think anyone purposely does a poor job. They either don't have the training they need to be excellent, or they don't see that their efforts are rewarded.

It is the job of the leader to take action to make sure everyone feels confident in their job tasks. People need to be challenged and their strengths need to be recognized. If you approach every problem and mistake in your center as a lack of training or information, you will be looking within to solve the problem instead of placing blame.

PROTIP: *Challenge your employees with figuring difficult tasks or performances. Recognize hard work and dedication publicly.*

The other benefit to training your staff is the natural motivation that comes from learning a new skill or idea. Learning motivates. Here are a few ways to get your staff the training they need, even if they don't know they need it:
- Bring in guest speakers
- Send staff to conferences
- Reward staff for reading books (related to what they are doing)
- Pay for staff to take online classes
- Pay for staff to take local trainings
- Organize staff retreats

Another problem that we face as far as training is that we often promote people out of their strength areas. We assume if someone is a great teacher that they will make a great director. Instead of promoting them out of their strengths, reward them with pay raises or other bonuses. Many of our clients have created career advancement strategies that don't include position changes. If teachers, directors, cooks, bus drivers, meet specific criteria to advance their job skills, they are rewarded with pay increases. I am not offering a specific scale because it will be different at every school and could possibly cause confusion. Some items to keep in mind if you want to create a pay scale or career ladder are experience, education, training certificates, goals met, additional roles performed (committee leader, volunteer, etc), and longevity at the school.

PROTIP: *Offer career advancement that doesn't include position change.*

We know that staff stay longer and do better in their positions the more they know. In turn, this keeps staff motivated. It is worth the pay increase to help staff expand their skills and allows for cross training in case the center is shorthanded. It will likely pay back your school 10-fold. Funding continuing education is often a double-edged sword because we are afraid we will invest the money and run the risk of the staff member leaving. What if you don't invest the money and they stay? Richard Branson is quoted saying *"Train your people well enough so they have the option to leave. Treat your people well enough that they don't want to leave."*

It is not necessarily your job to find professional development training for all of your staff. Put it on them to find wat they want to learn more about. The training they request should be in line with their goals. The same training may not motivate every single staff member, especially if they are not passionate about the subject. One easy way to help develop your staff is to reward them for reading. Just as you picked up this book (and hopefully found some easy and helpful action items), your staff can do the same and get motivated about subjects that are near and dear to them. Maybe they have a child who might be on the autism spectrum and reading will help them better benefit that child in the classroom.

"Those who don't read barely have an advantage over those who can't." – Verne Harnish

Reading is very literally the most inexpensive staff development and training you can offer to your employees. It's also a huge motivator. Reading child development articles and books to get new ideas to implement is a huge re-energizer for your staff. It can also help on-board your staff with new ideas and values you want to implement in your center. I shouldn't have to tell this group that it also improves vocabulary and communication all while reducing stress.

PROTIP: *Encourage and reward your staff for reading.*

Here are a few tips to help get your staff reading:

Refer to great books you've read in context.

Talk about ideas you've learned about from books. Don't just refer to a book, "Seven Habits of Highly Effective People changed my life, you should read it." Instead, point out what you learned from it. "I think at this staff meeting we should start with the end in mind; I was reading about it in The 7 Habits of Highly Effective People and I think it makes so much sense."

Purchase a great book for all staff members.

If there is particularly motivating book you've read and you really want your staff to read it, buy them a hard copy. Start conversation topics with your staff about points in the book to encourage them to open it.

Start a semi-formal book club.

If you really need your staff to read a book to understand your values and/or where you want to go in the future, start a semi-formal book club. It can be at a staff meeting or after hours. If you do it at a staff meeting, have it be short increments – let's discuss chapter 1 the first 15 minutes of our Wednesday staff meeting. Splitting it up like this will not overwhelm your staff, and others can read ahead of if they want.

Have books available for check out.

Have a library available for your staff. Buying books is not an expense many of them want to take on. Have a library available, or as bonuses, hand out Kindles or Nooks.

Give your staff time to read. One of the biggest excuses we hear about reading is "I don't have time." This one might be challenging, but if there is ever down time – nap time, opening, closing, that your center is at ratio, but you don't want to send staff home, let them go to an office and read. If this just isn't possible in your center, skip it. Or consider that paying someone an extra hour of time to read, might be inexpensive staff development.

Reward your staff for reading. Vern Harnish, author of *Scaling Up,* suggests having a reward system in place to encourage and reward staff for reading. Have staff members write down 2-5 take-a- ways from what they've read. Reward them with money, gift cards, or points for each book they read. There is actually an online tool to help with this called betterbookclub.com. This might be the better alternative to giving them time at work, because they are being rewarded for using their own time. Double bonus if you do both.

Subscribe to relevant journals and magazines.

Be sure to subscribe to The Young Child, Child Care Exchange, and other NAEYC or value specific articles (Reggio, Montessori, etc). These are quicker and easier reads than books, but can have a wealth of knowledge and keep your staff progressive.

Send out interesting and thought provoking blogs.

Hopefully our weekly Ezine is one of them you're sending. :)
Even if it's not, there are tons of great early childhood blogs. Google
Teacher Tom, Let the Children Play, Not Just Cute for some starting
points. You can send these out to your staff when they have great
articles. Hint: also follow these groups on Facebook so you know when
the material is fresh.

Here is a list of books we recommend for leaders in the Early
Childhood Field. Please note this list is ever growing and changing
because we are firm believers in staying progressive and "fresh" in the
field.
- *The Ultimate Child Care Marketing Guide* – Kris Murray
- *The 77 Best Strategies to Grow Your Child Care or Preschool Business*
  – Kris Murray
- *Child Care Marketing Online* – Devin Murray
- *Strengths Finder* – Tom Rath
- *Strengths Based Leadership* – Tom Rath, Barry Conchie
- *5 Languages of Appreciation* – Gary Chapman & Paul White
- *Built on Values* – Ann Rhoades
- *Seven Habits of Highly Effective People* – Stephen Covey
- *Scaling Up* – Verne Harnish
- *Leaders Eat Last* – Simon Sinek
- *Who Moved my Cheese* – Spencer Johnson
- *The Art of Awareness* – Margie Carter & Deb Curtis
- *The Visionary Director* – Deb Curtis & Margie Carter

Anything by:
- Margie Carter
- Deb Curtis
- Stephen Covey
- Lilian Katz
- Mimi Brodsky Chenfield
- Magda Gerber
- Dr. T. Berry Brazelton

In his book, *Scaling Up*, Verne Harnish says "The only way to 10x your business is to 10x the people in it." If you think about it, most college courses are basically a book club with work sheets and tests – why wouldn't we want to continually educate ourselves and our staff? Some of the most interesting staff meetings I have attended have been talking about a book we all agreed to read. People take away different points and have different strengths in implementation. I promise you will be surprised with what your team can come up with. Verne also notes *"If everyone in your company read one book per month, twelve a year, you will be 99% ahead of your competition."*

There is one last aspect to staff retention that we need to cover. The final chapter is about letting go of staff members.

ACTION STEPS:

- Look at your staff's goals to identify common areas that need training and resources.
- Look at staff evaluation to identify common areas that need more training and resources.
- Identify helpful books or articles to help staff with issues they may be having with children, families or other staff members.
- Ask your staff members their favorite books dealing with early childhood and leader. Consider starting or adding to your existing library.

CHAPTER TWELVE
WHEN TO LET GO

It may seem funny that a chapter on letting go of employees is placed within Part 2: Retaining Staff; however, it is a retention tool as well. I mentioned in the beginning of Part 2 that staff leave managers, which is true, but staff also leave co-workers. All too often we lose our A Players, because we keep our C & D Players on board too long. Guess which ones have more options to leave on their own?

If you have a staff member you need to remove, you likely know who it is. The challenge is actually letting them go. In this industry, we all have big hearts and have become entrenched in 5 or more chapters on how to mold your staff into wonderful employees who want to stay forever. Unfortunately, your efforts will be cut short if you let a bad fit poison the well. Each and every child care owner will hire someone who just doesn't fit within the company's values, often they will naturally weed themselves out if you are following every other step in this book.

Time and time again, I have people tell me that they let one "bad apple" stay until all of their other great employees left. By that time, these actions negatively impacted not only your staff retention rate, but your company culture as well. When it comes to letting go of employees, you want to set yourself up for success. As you may have noticed throughout this book, I have never claimed to be a lawyer, so please consult your lawyer on preferred termination policies. I am going to guide you through the process, but please make sure in your own state what practices you need to follow before letting someone go. Consider unemployment and other lawsuits, but do not be afraid to let someone go. Most states are "at will" states of employment. For

PROTIP: *Let staff members know what would constitute them being replaced in your organization.*

more information on how toxic a bad staff member can be to your entire organization read Vern Mason's book "Don't Go."

Other times we don't have a "bad apple", we just have someone who is not competent, stale, just "doesn't get it", has been with you forever, or is a great person, but not great at the job that we let stay for too long. These are often the hardest people to get rid of, they may not be causing noticeable damage to your organization or giving you push back, but they aren't contributing either. I would say give these people 6-12 months of goal setting and training to improve or try and move them to another role within your organization. If that doesn't work, you will need to replace with an "A" employee as well.

The first thing you want to consider within your organization is what criteria you consider constitutes a bad fit. Once this is defined, let everyone know. It will actually encourage job security when you tell employees "We will never consider firing you unless you are knowingly endangering a child or another employee, if you lie or steal, or if you undermine another employee's efforts; everything else is a training issue." Our client, Paul Huff, tells his employees this at staff meetings and it really helps them open up and participate. This sentence alones instills job security as well as clearly sets boundaries and expectations for the center. It also gives your employees a sense of relief that they will work with willing team members and they don't have to have "watch their back."

If you are holding your employees accountable for their actions, identifying opportunities for improvement, and setting genuine goals, letting an employee go should be a very easy decision. They either are not meeting their marks, or they do something that requires immediate termination. Do NOT keep these employees around on 2nd, 3rd, or 4th chances. Have a system in place so that it is clear to employees what constitutes reasons for termination. If you start giving out

PROTIP: *Let staff who are not making your center great find somewhere they will be happier.*

multiple chances or 'tries" your other employees will catch on and will no longer feel safe in their work environment.

We also have a fear of hiring that tricks us into hanging on to undesirable employees. Honestly, your employees would rather pick up the slack for a short period of time rather than work with a toxic person. If you are following everything in this book up to this point, you should be set up for success in that you will be able to hire someone competent to replace the person who needs to leave. If you are constantly using online and offline tactics to send people to your amazing careers page, you should be able to grab for a pool of qualified applicants. At that point you can go through your hiring process to hire the person who is the best fit for your culture and the skills you are looking for and by following the TRUST model for retention and letting go of toxic people, you should maintain your A Players. Happy teachers are your key to a successful child care program. Here at Child Care Marketing Solutions, we like to say that Happy Teachers = Happy Children= Happy Parents.

ACTION STEPS:

- Identify what qualities aren't a fit in your organization.
- Write down what reasons would constitute you terminating an employee immediately.
- Write down any poor employees. Start thinking of replacement strategy and compiling documentation for them to be let go.
- Contact your lawyer about employee termination and severance packages that are legal in your state.
- Identify any employees you don't love and decide what training could help you love them.

SUGGESTED READING:

- Read Vernon Mason's *Don't Go.*

FINAL THOUGHTS

This book was designed to be short and sweet and to the point to help put you on the fast track to staffing success. However, we never want you to feel overwhelmed. While all of the steps complement each other, if you feel like you have too much to do, the first thing you can do is survey your staff to see how your current cultural climate ranks.

Start writing down ideas you have and want to implement. Create steps for each process and put them in order of priority. Remember the goal is to have all "A players" on your team. Can you get rid of some people now? Or do you need to hire some people first, that will help with your direction. If you're not finding qualified people or "A players" I would definitely look at where you are searching for applicants first.

Remember, there are no "quick fixes" and this process takes time, sometimes even 6-12 months before you see a difference. Sometimes things get a little harder before they get easier, but what if you would have started a year ago?

Thanks for reading and if you would like more coaching or support from us at Child Care Marketing Solutions, be sure to check out child care-marketing.com. We have products and coaching available. Be sure to read about the Child Care Success Academy. This is our group of Child Care Owners and directors who come together to network and get one on one coaching from Kris Murray and myself. Everything you just read is much easier to implement if you have support.

Remember, the happier your staff is, the more quality you're offering your children and families.

Happy teachers = happy children = happy parents.

APPENDIX A
TEACHER INTERVIEW QUESTIONS

OPEN ENDED QUESTIONS TO GET TO KNOW CANDIDATE

- What events or influences from your childhood shaped who you are today?
- Tell me 2 or 3 things of which you are most proud.
- Tell me about a time when the odds were stacked against you but you overcame them and succeeded.
- What was your favorite book as a child?
- What job have you had in the past was your absolute favorite and why?
- What was your least favorite job and why?
- What do you do when you don't know the answer to a question?
- What qualities do you find most irritating in other people? How do you deal with it?

SCENARIOS

- The phone is ringing, there's someone at the door, the toilet is overflowing, a teacher just vomited. What do you do?
- You have a child in your room who can't speak English and cries constantly for 5 days straight. What do you do?
- You feel like a child in your classroom has a developmental delay or learning disability, what do you do?
- Tell me about a time when you helped resolve a particularly difficult conflict with your co-workers or clients.
- Describe a time when you went above and beyond the call of duty at work.

CULTURALLY BASED INTERVIEW QUESTIONS

• What are your thoughts on Technology in the classroom?
(Progressive, Traditional, Waldorf, Reggio, Montessori, Child-Led)
• When is the best time to teach a child to tie their shoe? How do you teach a child to tie their shoe?
(Progressive, Traditional, Waldorf, Reggio, Montessori, Child-Led)
• Tell me about a time you had a parent upset and you couldn't give them what they wanted. How did you handle the situation?
(Parents as Partners, Positivity, Communication, Integrity, Collaboration, Customer-First)
• Tell me about a time you had two children who were best friends, but fought a lot, how did you handle the situation?
(Parents as Partners, Positivity, Communication, Integrity, Collaboration, Progressive, Traditional, Child-Led, Fun, Loving, Kind)
• Tell me about a time you had a child with aggression, what steps did you take to set the child up to be successful?
(Parents as Partners, Positivity, Communication, Integrity, Collaboration, Progressive, Traditional, Child-Led, Fun, Loving, Kind)
• Why did you leave (want to leave) your last (current) position?
(Positivity, Communication, Integrity, Professional)
• Tell me about a time you had a child cry every morning at drop off?
(Parents as Partners, Positivity, Communication, Integrity, Collaboration, Progressive, Traditional, Child-Led, Fun, Loving, Kind)
• Have you ever worked with someone who was negative? How did you handle that?
(Positivity, Communication, Integrity, Collaboration, Fun, Loving, Kind)
• Have you ever been negative in a working environment? What did you learn from it?
(Positivity, Communication, Integrity, Collaboration, Fun,

Loving, Kind, Professional)
• Have you ever witnessed a co-worker breaking the rules, either knowingly or unknowingly? What did you do?
(**Positivity, Communication, Integrity, Collaboration, Fun, Loving, Kind, Professional**)
• Have you ever broken the rules or licensing standards because you felt it was in the best interest of a child or classroom?
(**Positivity, Communication, Integrity, Fun, Loving, Kind, Progressive**)

STRENGTHS-BASED MANAGEMENT QUESTIONS

• What do you feel is the best way for you to learn about the culture of our center?
• What motivates you the most in the classroom?
• Tell me about a time when you were on fire for your job?
• Tell me about a time when your energy was completely drained after work?

APPENDIX B
90 DAY STAFF RETENTION PLAN

IMMEDIATELY UPON HIRING

- Welcome to our family – Welcome Card, Letter, or Email from Owner sent when someone gets hired. Video or Document outlining your vision. If there is a separate director or direct supervisor, letter from them.
- Virtual introduction to mentor – introduce via email and give information about each party.
- What to expect your first day – Email outlining what they should bring the first day and what they will be covering. Will they be training

DAY 1

- Welcome Packet – Can include letters from students and other teachers, logo'd items such as mug, water glass, key chain, starbucks gift card, flowers, etc.
- Lunch catered in for staff in honor of new employee
- Direct supervisor phone call in evening to see how day went.
- Half Day of filling out paperwork and watching training videos
- Half Day observing classroom or spent with supervisor answering questions

WEEK 1

- Observation first 2 days
- Next 2 days – in classroom with extra support
- End of week follow up:
  > One-Hour meeting at the end of the week.
  > Email Friday at end of day or evening
  > Summarize the points the teacher should have picked up during the week. Answer any questions they might have.

WEEK 2
- Training Videos/Emails
- Email check in from Owner/Director
    What's going well?
    What could we improve?

ONE -MONTH ANNIVERSARY
- Hand written thank you from director/owner

90 DAY REVIEW
- Based on Core Values, knowledge of Policies, Interactions with families
- Goals for next 6 -9 months
- Business Cards

DATE-SPECIFIC DURING YEAR ONE
- Birthday Card -Signed by teacher(s), director and owner
- 6 month Testimonial Request – ask the teacher to write a testimonial on term of employment

ONE-YEAR ANNIVERSARY OF ENROLLMENT
- One Year Thank You for the Year Letter
- One Year 360 review
- Goals for next year
- Professional Development Plan

OTHER RELATED BLOG POSTS
BY JESSICA JOHNSEN

If you haven't already, join the conversation at childcare-marketing.com. Here are a three staff-related blogs you might have missed by Jessica Johnsen.

The True Cost of Employee Turnover
By: Jessica Johnsen

I started out to write this blog about the true cost of employee turnover. I wanted to be able to give you a tangible equation to figure out how to find out how much it costs your organization to lose an employee. Let me tell you, there is no easy tangible equation for this.

I have probably done more research for this blog than any other blog I've written. I've read dozens of articles online and white papers and scoured all my leadership and staffing books to find an easy equation. It doesn't exist and the data is all over the board.

Many books and articles suggest that on average it's two years of the employee's salary to hire and train the replacement. While that seems about right for higher level administration, it seems way too high for your more transient positions such as assistant teachers or floaters.

A couple articles that I read, broke the percentages down by the type of job.

This article **Employee-Retention-The-Real-Cost-of-Losing-an-Employee,** took research from the Center for American Progress (CAP) which suggested that it's a 16% of annual salary for low-paying high turnover jobs, 20% of annual salary for mid-range positions, and up to 213% annual salary for high educated positions. This article **What-was-leadership-thinking-the-shockingly-high-cost-of-employee-turnover** using newer data from Forbes suggests that the cost is even higher, 30-50% annual salary for high turnover, low-paying positions, 150% of annual salary for mid-range positions, and 400% for higher paying positions.

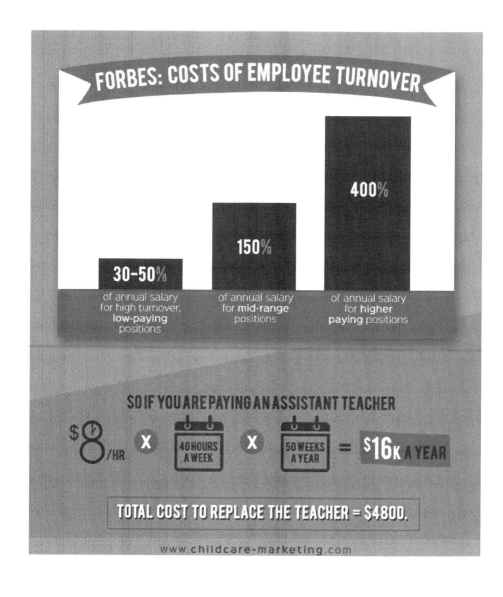

Given the variables that we face in the industry I would guess that the second numbers are closer to accurate. So, if you are paying an assistant teacher $8/hour, 40 hours a week, for 50 weeks a year, they would be making around 16K a year. If we use the lower end of the scale and take that times 30% that would mean it costs around $4,800 to replace that teacher.

Why is the cost so high? Here are the factors that go into replacing an employee that are costing you money. Unfortunately, in our industry, there are so many other factors that are effected by employee turnover that I cannot put a value on.

- **Cost of Hiring New Employees** – paying for ads, your hourly time spent looking over applicants and interviewing, running background checks, and any other costs associated with the interview process.

- **Cost of training new employees** – paying your new employee to learn, paying either yourself or another person to spend time training, paying a 3rd person to cover the classroom while the new person is training.

- **Cost of lost productivity** – not only are you paying wages to hire and train new employees, you're also missing out on time and potential revenue of that time spent elsewhere. If you are spending all of your time interviewing, or on of your directors is spending a lot of time training, when they could be working on parent relations or other high pay off activities, it is really costing you a lot more than you think. This is also the cost of training and workshops you sent the previous employer too. Did they have music training that you now won't have at your center or a special way of getting the children to potty train?

- **Cost of lost motivation among others** – You're also secretly paying for the loss of motivation to others who have to pick up the slack of the missing employee. In our amazing, but challenging industry, this cost cannot be underestimated. Burnout is high and can lead to more turnover, which would then put you at the top of this list again.

- **Potential loss of parents** – We can't ignore that you also might lose some revenue in the process of hiring and training new employees. There are two ways this can happen. One is that parents leave because a particular person that they had a relationship with has left. The second is that parents start to leave because of the chaos that is caused by many teachers coming and going.

- **Potential disruption to children's learning** – although we do our very best to make sure that transitions are seamless and painless to the children, any transition can be hard on the children.

Hopefully this article isn't all doom and gloom for you, but **it is important to realize how much it does cost you to have high turnover.** It doesn't mean you should keep toxic employees around for fear of this cost, because that can be even more costly. It also doesn't mean you should quit running ads all the time or pay less for them, that payoff is much higher if you get a great person.

It **DOES** mean that you now have more knowledge in your toolbox. It **DOES** mean that you should take an extra minute today and every day to thank your existing staff. It also means that you should really look at why people are leaving and see if there is anything that can be fixed sooner than later.

Remember, relationships are TWO people, and if you have a lot of staff leaving, there it is only the symptom of a bigger problem.

Top Tips For Professional Staff Development
By Jessica Johnsen

Professional development in the early childhood education field has been a hot topic lately.

In most states continuing education units (CEUs) are required. How many CEUs are required per year depends on your state and what qualifies as a CEU depends on not only the state, but also your individual licensing consultant. **Talk with your licensing specialist to find out what is accepted in your state.**

Keep in mind that there is a difference between early childhood professional development and team building activities, but often there can be overlap, and that's a huge bonus.

I suggest you look for overlap as often as possible to help your professional development budget at your child care business.

For instance, **group yoga, pilates, or zumba, team dinners with a specific topic, and group outings to public places such as art museums can often be passed off as professional development because you are gaining information that can be taken back to the classroom.** Just print out a certificate and have someone sign off on the training. Some licensing specialists are stricter and will not let this pass & some states require CEU's to be authorized by a particular agency, but it's worth asking.**Group activities like this are a fantastic way to build team culture and it doesn't require staff to double dip in the personal time and it doesn't require you to double dip in your budget.**

Beyond the child care training activities I just talked about, **providing professional development for your child care staff can be confusing and a slippery slope.** Do you pay for all professional development? Do you provide it all in house? If you pay for Sally to go to a state conference, do you pay for Susie's class? What about staff members who get motivation from learning and want to attend every class and training possible? Do directors get to go to more than teachers? Is it even possible to provide it all in house?

Do staff have to take PTO to attend weekday training? Do you pay them for their time if they attend a training? Do you pay gas and mileage? Again, in states such as California, you may not have a choice on many of these questions.

There likely isn't a one size fits all answer to your professional development and child care training needs. But I really want you to take away some ideas from this blog about providing professional development for your teachers & leaders that not only meets requirements but also provides your staff with invaluable information and motivation.

Professional development in early childhood is so important, so the idea is not just to meet the requirements, but for your staff to change mindset, behavior, or classroom procedures.

Too often we offer conference registration and trainings simply so that we can add a certificate to a file and pass inspection. We haphazardly choose inexpensive state conference that are on weekends without looking at classes offered. If chosen thoughtfully, **professional development for your child care staff can truly be life changing and re-energizing, especially during times of high teacher burn out.**

Paying for staff development can actually help you reduce staff turnover, which can end up saving you money.

The trick with choosing successful professional development & training is to **find a balance of topics for each staff member that helps them capitalize on their strengths and run damage control on their weaknesses.**

Too often, you may see "areas of need" and try to get staff training in those areas. If not paired with interesting topics for your child care staff, only meeting the "areas of need" that you diagnose can actually back fire. **Staff will begin to see professional development as boring and somewhat reprimanding.**

For instance, if you have a staff member who loves music and movement activities in her classroom, but she isn't the best about communicating with parents, you might see the need to get her more training in communication or parent relationships. It would be best to find a combination of training, "how to tell parents about the importance of music and movement" or find a conference that offers trainings on both subjects.

It works the same for your entire child care staff. If you find that you have a staff that is guilty of gossip (and whose staff isn't at some point?), it is probably better to have team building exercises than to bring someone in to talk about the dangers of gossip. That message would be much better received if everyone is getting along and you don't have much gossip. That way it's preventative and not making anyone feel defensive.

So how do you know **what trainings are best for each staff member and what trainings the whole team will benefit from?**

The easiest answer to this is to ask your staff. I am including an easy-to-use sheet that you can modify or use as is to know what your staff would benefit from most. You want to know what your staff really love about their jobs and what they don't love so much. You'll want to find out what their favorite activity with the children is and what activities or behaviors they find challenging.

Here are some more ideas when planning your early childhood staff development:

- Have a yearly staff development calendar to avoid spending money at the last minute.

- Have a set dollar amount for any child care trainings that your staff wants to attend that are not in house.

- Have staff members give a short summary to the whole staff of all trainings/classes/events they attend out of house.

- Determine great, cost effective conferences that a lot of staff members can go to and let them know ahead of time.

- Have staff go to the conference with a plan of what breakouts they will attend and how each breakout will meet their set goals.

- Encourage staff to participate in contests with each other to earn funding for out of state or large conferences. (I.e. Classrooms with no tardiness or unexcused absences will be entered into a drawing to go to the NAEYC conference.)

- Have staff pay you back 50% of the conference fee if they leave within a year of attending.

- Provide a dollar amount towards conferences and trainings for each year the employee has been with you. For instance, every gets $100 base and $25 for each year they have worked at the school.

- Utilize local resources such as museums, community gardens, and health consultants to provide training for your staff.

- Think out of the box. Could you do a painting class, yoga class, cooking class, sign language seminar as a fun group activity that will count towards professional development?

Remember staff development can seem costly, but educated, progressive, motivated, energetic, and happy staff will pay you back 10-fold.

4 Ways To Motivate Staff And Get Their Buy In
By Jessica Johnsen

One of my biggest motivators is learning new ideas and finding new ways to do things. It gives me energy and I almost bubble over with excitement waiting to actually be able to share or implement those ideas. I know I'm not alone on this. I see our members take away pages of to-do lists and hundreds of ideas from our live academy meetings as well as the Child Care Success Summit. Unfortunately, the road block is often that your new ideas can seem draining to your staff and teachers, the exact people you need to help implement or carry out those ideas.

There are a couple reasons this can be a road block. One, your staff may be doing all they can do to get through the day implementing the *old* ideas they've been asked to carry out. Two, your staff might not see the reasoning on *why* they need to change what they are doing or adding another step.

Here are four ways to pass your motivation on to your staff in a way that inspires them so they have the same drive.

1.**Get buy in** *before* **demanding an idea be implemented.** This can be challenging as we all want to check items off of our to-do list as fast as possible. The problem is, we delegate our ideas as task items instead of as ideas with purpose. Whoever is carrying out that task, often has the goal of merely completing the said task. They do it with little heart or emotion just to get it done, which means it isn't really carried out to the expectation of the original person. We run into this when owners are trying to get their directors to implement the phone script or change up their tour. It makes a huge difference if you record a phone conversation of the director with a potential new parent and have them listen to the call. Hearing themselves, they might be able to point out areas where they sound in a hurry or give out rates too fast. Then they realize that studying the phone script and making it their own has an advantage.

2. **Give information about the** *context* **of where the idea came from.** Again, this comes when we put our motivation into a check list. We don't pass along the motivation part, just the check list. If you give the context of the situation where you got the idea, it gains your employees buy in as well.

The more details you can give, the better.

Kris and Camille recently came back from the Titanium Meeting (Kris' mastermind group) and I knew that they were going to be full of new ideas and direction for the company. While nothing can replace being somewhere in person, it's important that the attendees are able to paint the picture for team members who weren't able to attend. Almost immediately, Kris did just this. She wrote out an email of all of her new ideas with details and context. It really helped start the conversation about what she learned during our team meeting.

The more you can share your ideas almost as if telling a story, the better. It might sound something like this.

"I went to a conference last week of all business owners, it was phenomenal, there were about 600 child care owners in the room. Kris Murray is on the stage and she was talking about how to recession proof your business. As she was talking, she was listing the 7 ways, 4 of which we are already doing (then name which 4), so I was really proud of our team. One thing we aren't doing, that other owners have had success with is having the teachers interact on the tour. One woman stood up and shared the story, that when she had her teachers start engaging with parents on the tour, she had a 50% increase in tour conversion, so if 10 people toured, 5 more enrolled on the spot. So if she was enrolling 3 out of every 10, now she is enrolling 6-8. That would make Sally Directors job so much easier and you all could start getting to know parent's sooner. As I was asking around, this is a common practice that really sets people apart. What do you guys think?" That probably goes over a lot better than "The person who ran the conference I went to says it is a good idea for teachers to talk to parents on the tour, start doing that."

3. Follow through, follow through, follow through. Did I mention follow through? Nothing is a bigger de-motivator than coming home with new ideas and trying to implement all of them at once and then letting some die out or fade away. Trust me, if you're always trying to implement new things and you don't keep them up for at least 6 months to a year, your staff will come to hate when you go to conferences or have new ideas at all. This is especially hard for people who are idea people. It is important for you to keep a list of ideas and then implement only the ones you know will be completed to entirety.

Make a plan for each idea with all of the steps and timeline. If you ask teachers to start talking to parents on the tour, have a staff meeting to train on what that looks like, then check back in with the staff each month to see how it's been going. Ask what it feels like for them, what they've been saying, and have them share with each other.

4. Have a place to share books or start an internal book club. About a year ago, I wrote an article on the easiest way to motivate your staff, which was through reading. It's still true, we gain so much knowledge through reading. I run into so many people who claim they don't read. I would say they haven't found the correct material. Have a variety of relevant journals, magazines, and books available in your library.

Keep in mind that people learn best and are most motivated to solve challenges they are facing. While you might be worried about enrollment, your teachers might be more worried about behavior management. Instead of you reading and telling them how to handle the situation, recommend great books and then give the staff member the book. They will be more likely to read it if they think it has answers they are seeking.

While I have a list of books recommended in the blog post mentioned above, some new ones that we recommend over here at **Child Care Marketing Solutions** are:

- *All In: How the Best Managers Create a Culture of Belief and Drive Big Results* – by Adrian Gostick and Chester Elton.

- *The One Thing: The Surprisingly Simple Truth Behind Extraordinary Results* – by Gary Keller and Jay Papasan

- *Uncontainable: How Passion, Commitment, and Conscious Capitalism Built a Business Where Everyone Thrives by* – Kip Tindell and Casey Shilling

- *Drive: The Surprising Truth About What Motivates Us* – by Daniel H. Pink.

PRODUCTS AND SERVICES
FROM CHILD CARE MARKETING SOLUTIONS

CHILD CARE SUCCESS ACADEMY

Gold Core Coaching Member:

As an owner-director, director, or start-up in the early learning field, Survival Sally (or Survival Sam) feels lost as she tries to manage her program and can't seem to figure out how to get OUT of Survival Mode. Her enrollment isn't growing as quickly as she'd like (or she doesn't have any enrollment yet as she's in start-up mode). She is unsure of how to market her program effectively, and how much time and money to spend on a marketing plan. Her cash-flow is extremely tight, and she may be working long hours because she can't afford to outsource important tasks. She may even be working in the classroom to save money on payroll.

Platinum VIP Coaching Member:

As the owner or executive director of a business in the child care industry, Multiplier Mary (or Multiplier Mike) is out of 'survival mode', but she still has huge challenges to overcome in order to grow her business and maintain her sanity. She feels pulled in many different directions by the needs of her staff, customer families, and the constant demands of business. She has a strong desire to grow her program to multiple locations, or even has a vision for a 'side business' related to the child care field. She has an entrepreneurial drive and wants to make an impact on her community, but she can't seem to get out of overwhelm in order to make her dreams a reality.

Diamond Elite Coaching Member:

As a seasoned child care business owner, Visionary Vicky (or Visionary Vince) has achieved substantial success and is proud of the business she's built. However, she knows there are strategies she could implement to make her business more successful, and to get more freedom in life. She wants to position her company for further growth, even franchising, and would like to be in a group of advancing peers whom she can learn and mastermind with. She feels overwhelmed by the lack of systems and consistent training of directors, and she'd love someone to take that over completely so she can focus on growth and perhaps even an exit strategy.

RECOMMENDED RESOURCES

ADRIAN GOSTICK & CHESTER ELTON:

All In: How the Best Managers Create a Culture of Belief and Drive Big Results

In the highest-performing teams and companies, managers create a "culture of belief," following seven essential steps of leadership.

To have any hope of succeeding as a manager, you need to get your people *all in.*

Whether you manage the smallest of teams or a multi-continent organization, you are the owner of a work culture—congratulations—and few things will have a bigger impact on your performance than getting your people to buy into your ideas and your cause and to believe what they do matters.

Bestselling authors of *The Carrot Principle* and *The Orange Revolution,* Adrian Gostick and Chester Elton return to answer the most overlooked leadership questions of our day: Why are some managers able to get their employees to commit wholeheartedly to their culture and give that extra push that leads to outstanding results? And how can managers at any level build and sustain a profitable, vibrant work-group culture of their own?

These leading workplace experts teamed up with research giant Towers Watson to analyze an unprecedented 300,000-person study, and they made a groundbreaking finding: managers of the highest-performing work groups create a "culture of belief." In these distinctive workplaces, people *believe* in their leaders and in the company's vision, values, and goals. Employees are not only engaged but also enabled and energized (termed the three Es), which leads to astonishing results—average annual revenues three times higher than for organizations lacking such a positive culture. And this was true during a period that included this most recent recession.

Based on their extensive consulting experience and in-depth interviews with leaders and employees at exceptional companies such as American Express, Cigna, Avis Budget, Pepsi Bottling, and Hard Rock, the authors present a simple seven-step road map for creating a culture of belief: define a burning platform; create a customer focus; develop agility; share everything; partner with your talent; root for each other; and establish clear accountability. Delving into specific how-tos for each step, they share eye-opening stories of exceptional leaders in action, vividly depicting just how these powerful methods can be implemented by any manager.

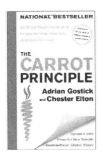

The Carrot Principle: How the Best Managers Use Recognition to Engage Their People, Retain Talent, and Accelerate Performance

Stick Management is out. Carrot management is in! *The Carrot Principle* offers proven strategies to help recognize and motivate your valued employees.

Since its original publication in 2007, the *New York Times* bestseller *The Carrot Principle* has received rave reviews in *The Wall Street Journal*, *Fortune*, and *The New York Times*, and has helped a host of managers to energize their teams, and companies to dramatically boost their business results. The book was even adopted by the prestigious FranklinCovey International training and consulting group for its leadership training. This updated edition couldn't come at a better time, as the economic downturn requires us all to come up with creative and cost-effective ways to stimulate growth and productivity.

Revealing the groundbreaking results of one of the most in-depth management studies ever undertaken, *The Carrot Principle* shows definitively that the central characteristic of the most successful managers is that they provide their employees with frequent and effective recognition. With independent results from HealthStream Research, and analysis by bestselling leadership experts Adrian Gostick and Chester Elton, this breakthrough study of 200,000 people over ten years found dramatically greater business results when managers offered constructive praise and meaningful rewards in ways that powerfully motivated employees to excel. These managers lead with carrots, not sticks, and in doing so achieve higher:

- Productivity
- Engagement
- Retention

In a new chapter, Gostick and Elton report on the results of an extensive study, conducted by leading research authority Towers Perrin, that confirms the extraordinary effectiveness of the Carrot Principle approach all around the globe.

Drawing on case studies from leading companies including Disney, DHL, KPMG, and Pepsi Bottling Group, Gostick and Elton show how the key to recognition *done right* is combining it with four other core traits of effective leadership. Gostick and Elton walk readers through exactly how to use the simple but powerful methods they have discovered all great managers use to provide their employees with this effective recognition, which can be learned easily and will produce immediate results.

Great recognition can be done in a matter of moments -- and it doesn't take budget-busting amounts of money. Following these simple steps will make you a high-performance leader and take your team to a new level of achievement.

What Motivates Me: Put Your Passions to Work

What Motivates Me will help readers align the work they do every day, for the rest of their lives, with what truly motivates them. It also includes a code to the Motivators Assessment. This is not a personality test, but a scientifically valid assessment that digs straight to the core of what motivates you at work. The book also features a set of thought-provoking exercises to help readers sculpt their jobs with 60 powerful strategies.

After analyzing the results of 850,000 interviews, the authors sought to discover why so many people are not as engaged and energized as they could be at work. They found those who are happiest and most successful are engaged in work that aligns with what motivates them. *What Motivates Me* offers an extensively tested method to help readers identify their core motivators and figure out the disconnects between their passions and their current work, and guides all those searching for joy and engagement by asking the important questions – "What motivates me?" and "What can I do about it?"

ANN RHOADES:

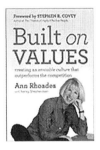

Built on Values: Creating an Enviable Culture that Outperforms the Competition

Most leaders know that a winning, engaged culture is the key to attracting top talent—and customers. Yet, it remains elusive *how* exactly to create this ideal workplace —one where everyone from the front lines to the board room knows the company's values and feels comfortable and empowered to act on them.

Based on Ann Rhoades' years of experience with JetBlue, Southwest, and other companies known for their trailblazing corporate cultures, *Built on Values* reveals exactly *how* leaders can create winning environments that allow their employees and their companies to thrive. Companies that create or improve values-based cultures can become higher performers, both in customer and employee satisfaction and financial return, as proven by Rhoades' work with JetBlue, Southwest Airlines, Disney, Loma Linda University Hospitals, Doubletree Hotels, Juniper Networks, and P.F. Chang's China Bistros.

Built on Values provides a clear blueprint for how to accomplish culture change, showing:

• How to exceed the expectations of employees and customers

- How to develop a Values Blueprint tailored to your organization's goals and put it into action

- Why it's essential to hire, fire, and reward people based on values alone

- How to establish a discipline for sustaining a values-centric culture

Built on Values helps companies get on the pathway to greatness by showing the exact steps for either curing an ailing company culture or creating a new one from scratch.

GARY CHAPMAN & PAUL WHITE:

The 5 Languages of Appreciation in the Workplace: Empowering Organizations by Encouraging People

The 5 Languages of Appreciation in the Workplace: Empowering Organizations by Encouraging People, by Gary Chapman and Paul White, applies the love language concept to the workplace. This book helps supervisors and managers effectively communicate appreciation and encouragement to their employees, resulting in higher levels of job satisfaction, healthier relationships between managers and employees, and decreased cases of burnout.

Ideal for both the profit and non-profit sectors, the principles presented in this book have a proven history of success in businesses, schools, medical offices, churches, and industry. Each book contains an access code for the reader to take a comprehensive online MBA Inventory (Motivating By Appreciation)—a $20 value.

The inventory is designed to provide a clearer picture of an individual's primary language of appreciation and motivation as experienced in a work-related setting. This assists managers and supervisors in communicating effectively to their team members, and thus building a more positive and productive work environment.

KRIS MURRAY:

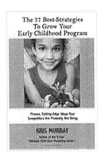

The 77 Best Strategies to Grow Your Early Childhood Program: Proven, Cutting-Edge Strategies Your Competitors Are Probably Not Using

The goal of this book is to hand you easy-to-implement ideas that can help you get fully enrolled in your early childhood program, with a waiting list. And not just any old ideas – these are the 77 BEST ideas and strategies we use consistently. Kris Murray has helped hundreds of owners grow their enrollment by 15 to 300 percent in just a few months, so it's possible for you too. In fact, she has included some of their case studies and results from using the ideas in this book, to provide you with proof and inspiration. Kris Murray's first book, "The Ultimate Child Care Marketing Guide", has sold thousands of copies and is 5-star rated on Amazon. Kris wrote this second book, as an easy-to-use idea generator for way to market your child care, daycare, or preschool. Anytime you need a boost in creativity for building enrollment, you can consult this book as your idea resource. Pick one or two ideas that appeal to you, and get started.

The Ultimate Child Care Marketing Guide: Tactics, Tools, and Strategies for Success

Proven marketing techniques for a more profitable child care business. You have the skills and expertise to provide high-quality care to children. Do you also know the best, most effective ways to market your child care program to prospective families? The Ultimate Child Care Marketing Guide is filled with exercises, action steps, and strategies to help you become a more business-savvy leader and entrepreneurial thinker. Built around the four pillars of marketing—metrics, market, message, and media—this resource will help you grow your child care business, whether you run a small program or large center. As you develop core marketing and business skills, you will be able to

- Track marketing activities to see which strategies work best for your program

- Identify and reach prospective families

- Understand the basic elements of creating and using a marketing plan

- Fill your program to capacity in any economic climate.

MARCUS BUCKINGHAM:

Now, Discover Your Strengths

The publication of *Now, Discover Your Strengths* in 2001 launched a worldwide strengths revolution. To date, more than 11 million people have discovered their strengths, and tens of thousands more are discovering theirs every week. **Gallup Press** has published numerous strengths-based books, and **Gallup Strengths Center** has become a worldwide destination for strengths-based development.

Since the book's release, Gallup has continued to dedicate countless hours to developing our strengths science, the brainchild of the late Dr. Donald O. Clifton, who was named Father of Strengths-Based Psychology by the American Psychological Association. Part of that investment resulted in Clifton StrengthsFinder 2.0 — a refined upgrade of the original assessment for discovering your strengths.

To ensure that you have the best possible experience in discovering and developing your strengths, we have made Clifton StrengthsFinder 2.0 available to those who purchase the electronic version of *Now, Discover Your Strengths*.

The updated assessment includes new reports and resources, including the Strengths Insight and Action-Planning Guide. This guide goes far beyond the standardized reports of the older assessment by providing you with personalized insight statements unique to your specific combination of strengths.

These highly customized Strengths Insights are an in-depth analysis of your top five strengths. They describe who you are in astonishing detail and provide you with a comprehensive understanding of yourself, your strengths and what makes you stand out.

These updated resources, in combination with *Now, Discover Your Strengths*, give you the best opportunity to soar with your strengths — at work and in your life.

MARGIE CARTER & DEB CURTIS:

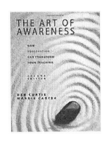

The Art of Awareness, Second Edition: How Observation Can Transform Your Teaching

The key to observing children, state authors Deb Curtis and Margie Carter in The Art of Awareness, is using observation as more than just a teaching technique. Observing children closely provides a new way of thinking about learning and teaching, a way of making children visible as they are, not just as we want them to be.

Observant teachers will find more than techniques for wtching or taking notes about children--they will discover a different way of being with children.

Featuring nine Observation Study Sessions, The Art of Awareness offers ideas, activities, and experiences--much more than just a set of checklists and facts to learn. Chapters cover seven different aspects of children's lives and how to observe them, as well as tips for gathering and preparing documentation.

Observation requires a commitment to systematic study and ongoing practice, write Curtis and Carter. The Art of Awareness is an inspiring and practical look at how to see the children in your care--and how to see what they see.

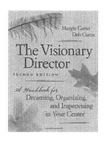

The Visionary Director, Second Edition: A Handbook for Dreaming, Organizing, and Improvising in Your Center

An inspiring and practical guide to creating a larger vision in early child care, this popular professional development tool has been thoroughly revised and offers a concrete framework for organizing an early childhood center director's ideas and work. Updated and expanded, it reflects new requirements and initiatives for center directors and addresses topics including cultivating a vision, developing "systems thinking" for management roles, implementing principles and strategies for mentoring, building a learning community for adults and children, and bringing visions to life. The Visionary Director provides directors with information to perform their jobs with motivation and creativity.

PATRICK LENCIONI:

The Five Dysfunctions of a Team: A Leadership Fable

In The Five Dysfunctions of a Team Patrick Lencioni once again offers a leadership fable that is as enthralling and instructive as his first two best-selling books, The Five Temptations of a CEO and The Four Obsessions of an Extraordinary Executive. This time, he turns his keen intellect and storytelling power to the fascinating, complex world of teams.

Kathryn Petersen, Decision Tech's CEO, faces the ultimate leadership crisis: Uniting a team in such disarray that it threatens to bring down the entire company. Will she succeed? Will she be fired? Will the company fail? Lencioni's utterly gripping tale serves as a timeless reminder that leadership requires as much courage as it does insight.

Throughout the story, Lencioni reveals the five dysfunctions which go to the very heart of why teams even the best ones-often struggle. He outlines a powerful model and actionable steps that can be used to overcome these common hurdles and build a cohesive, effective team. Just as with his other books, Lencioni has written a compelling fable with a powerful yet deceptively simple message for all those who strive to be exceptional team leaders.

Overcoming the Five Dysfunctions of a Team: A Field Guide for Leaders, Managers, and Facilitators

In the years following the publication of Patrick Lencioni's best-seller The Five Dysfunctions of a Team, fans have been clamoring for more information on how to implement the ideas outlined in the book. In Overcoming the Five Dysfunctions of a Team, Lencioni offers more specific, practical guidance for overcoming the Five Dysfunctions—using tools, exercises, assessments, and real-world examples. He examines questions that all teams must ask themselves: Are we really a team? How are we currently performing? Are we prepared to invest the time and energy required to be a great team? Written concisely and to the point, this guide gives leaders, line managers, and consultants alike the tools they need to get their teams up and running quickly and effectively.

SIMON SINEK

Leaders Eat Last: Why Some Teams Pull Together and Others Don't

Why do only a few people get to say "I love my job"? It seems unfair that finding fulfillment at work is like winning a lottery; that only a few lucky ones get to feel valued by their organizations, to feel like they belong.

Imagine a world where almost everyone wakes up inspired to go to work, feels trusted and valued during the day, then returns home feeling fulfilled.

This is not a crazy, idealized notion. Today, in many successful organizations, great leaders are creating environments in which people naturally work together to do remarkable things.

In his travels around the world since the publication of his bestseller Start with Why, Simon Sinek noticed that some teams were able to trust each other so deeply that they would literally put their lives on the line for each other. Other teams, no matter what incentives were offered, were doomed to infighting, fragmentation and failure. Why?

The answer became clear during a conversation with a Marine Corps general.

"Officers eat last," he said.

Sinek watched as the most junior Marines ate first while the most senior Marines took their place at the back of the line. What's symbolic in the chow hall is deadly serious on the battlefield: great leaders sacrifice their own comfort—even their own survival—for the good of those in their care.

This principle has been true since the earliest tribes of hunters and gatherers. It's not a management theory; it's biology. Our brains and bodies evolved to help us find food, shelter, mates and especially safety. We've always lived in a dangerous world, facing predators and enemies at every turn. We thrived only when we felt safe among our group.

Our biology hasn't changed in fifty thousand years, but our environment certainly has. Today's workplaces tend to be full of cynicism, paranoia and self-interest. But the best organizations foster trust and cooperation because their leaders build what Sinek calls a Circle of Safety that separates the security inside the team from the challenges outside.

The Circle of Safety leads to stable, adaptive, confident teams, where everyone feels they belong and all energies are devoted to facing the common enemy and seizing big opportunities.

As he did in Start with Why, Sinek illustrates his ideas with fascinating true stories from a wide range of examples, from the military to manufacturing, from government to investment banking.

The biology is clear: when it matters most, leaders who are willing to eat last are rewarded with deeply loyal colleagues who will stop at nothing to advance their leader's vision and their organization's interests. It's amazing how well it works.

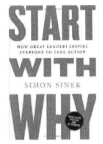

Start with Why: How Great Leaders Inspire Everyone to Take Action

Simon Sinek is leading a movement to build a world in which the vast majority of us are inspired by the work we do. Millions have already seen his video on TED.com about the importance of knowing why we do what we do. *Start with Why* takes the concept even deeper.

Any person or organization can explain *what* they do; some can explain *how* they are different or better; but very few can clearly articulate *why*. **WHY** is not about money or profit – those are results. **WHY** is the thing that inspires us and inspires those around us. From Martin Luther King, Jr. to Steve Jobs to the Wright Brothers, *Start with Why* shows that the leaders who inspire all think, act, and communicate in the exact same way – and it's the complete opposite of what everyone else does. Drawing on a wide range of real-life stories, it provides a framework upon which organizations can be built, movements can be led, and people can be inspired – and it all starts with **WHY**.

SPENCER JOHNSON:

Who Moved My Cheese?: An Amazing Way to Deal with Change in Your Work and in Your Life

With Who Moved My Cheese? Dr. Spencer Johnson realizes the need for finding the language and tools to deal with change--an issue that makes all of us nervous and uncomfortable.

Most people are fearful of change because they don't believe they have any control over how or when it happens to them. Since change happens either to the individual or by the individual, Spencer Johnson shows us that what matters most is the attitude we have about change.

When the Y2K panic gripped the corporate realm before the new millenium, most work environments finally recognized the urgent need to get their computers and other business systems up to speed and able to deal with unprecedented change. And businesses realized that this was not enough: they needed to help people get ready, too.

Spencer Johnson has created his new book to do just that. The coauthor of the multimillion bestseller The One Minute Manager has written a deceptively simple story with a dramatically important message that can radically alter the way we cope with change. Who Moved My Cheese? allows for common themes to become topics for discussion and individual interpretation.

Who Moved My Cheese? takes the fear and anxiety out of managing the future and shows people a simple way to successfully deal with the changing times, providing them with a method for moving ahead with their work and lives safely and effectively.

STEPHEN COVEY:

The 7 Habits of Highly Effective People: Powerful Lessons in Personal Change

The 7 Habits of Highly Effective People: Powerful Lessons in Personal Change was a groundbreaker when it was first published in 1990, and it continues to be a business bestseller with more than 10 million copies sold. Stephen Covey, an internationally respected leadership authority, realizes that true success encompasses a balance of personal and professional effectiveness, so this book is a manual for performing better in both arenas. His anecdotes are as frequently from family situations as from business challenges. Before you can adopt the seven habits, you'll need to accomplish what Covey calls a "paradigm shift"--a change in perception and interpretation of how the world works. Covey takes you through this change, which affects how you perceive and act regarding productivity, time management, positive thinking, developing your "proactive muscles" (acting with initiative rather than reacting), and much more. This isn't a quick-tips-start-tomorrow kind of book. The concepts are sometimes intricate, and you'll want to study this book, not skim it. When you finish, you'll probably have Post-it notes or hand-written annotations in every chapter, and you'll feel like you've taken a powerful seminar by Covey.

STEPHEN M. R. COVEY:

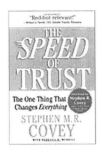

The SPEED of TRUST: The One Thing That Changes Everything

Stephen M.R. Covey shows how trust—and the speed at which it is established with clients and, employees—is essential to a successful organization.

With nearly 750,000 copies in print, this instant classic shows that establishing trust is "the one thing that changes everything" (Marcus Buckingham, coauthor of Now, Discover Your Strengths) in both business and life.

Trust, says Stephen M.R. Covey, is the very basis of the new global economy, and he shows how trust—and the speed at which it is established with clients, employees, and constituents—is the essential ingredient for any high–performance, successful organization.

For business leaders and public figures in any arena, The Speed of Trust offers an unprecedented and eminently practical look at exactly how trust functions in our every transaction and relationship—from the most personal to the broadest, most indirect interaction—and how to establish trust immediately so that you and your organization can forego the time–killing, bureaucratic check–and–balance processes so often deployed in lieu of actual trust.

TOM RATH:

StrengthsFinder 2.0

Do you have the opportunity to do what you do best every day?

Chances are, you don't. All too often, our natural talents go untapped. From the cradle to the cubicle, we devote more time to fixing our shortcomings than to developing our strengths.

To help people uncover their talents, Gallup introduced the first version of its online assessment, StrengthsFinder, in 2001 which ignited a global conversation and helped millions to discover their top five talents.

In its latest national bestseller, StrengthsFinder 2.0, Gallup unveils the new and improved version of its popular assessment, language of 34 themes, and much more (see below for details). While you can read this book in one sitting, you'll use it as a reference for decades.

Loaded with hundreds of strategies for applying your strengths, this new book and accompanying website will change the way you look at yourself-- and the world around you--forever.

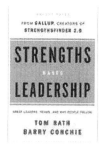

Strengths Based Leadership: Great Leaders, Teams, and Why People Follow

From the author of the long-running #1 bestseller *StrengthsFinder 2.0* comes a landmark study of great leaders, teams and the reasons why people follow.

Nearly a decade ago, Gallup unveiled the results of a landmark 30-year research project that ignited a global conversation on the topic of strengths. More than 3 million people have since taken Gallup's StrengthsFinder assessment, which forms the core of several books on this topic, including the #1 international bestseller *StrengthsFinder 2.0.*

In recent years, while continuing to learn more about strengths, Gallup scientists have also been examining decades of data on the topic of leadership. They studied more than 1 million work teams, conducted more than 20,000 in-depth interviews with leaders and even interviewed more than 10,000 followers around the world to ask exactly *why* they followed the most important leader in their life.

In *Strengths Based Leadership*, #1 *New York Times* bestselling author Tom Rath and renowned leadership consultant Barry Conchie reveal the results of this research. Based on their discoveries, the book identifies three keys to being a more effective leader: knowing your strengths and investing in others' strengths, getting people with the right strengths on your team, and understanding and meeting the four basic needs of those who look to you for leadership.

As you read *Strengths Based Leadership*, you'll hear firsthand accounts from some of the most successful organizational leaders in recent history, from the founder of Teach For America to the president of The Ritz-Carlton, as they discuss how their unique strengths have driven their success. Filled with novel research and actionable ideas, *Strengths Based Leadership* will give you a new road map for leading people toward a better future.

A unique access code allows you to take a new leadership version of Gallup's StrengthsFinder program. The new version of this program provides you with specific strategies for leading with your top five strengths and enables you to plot the strengths of your team based on the four domains of leadership strength revealed in the book.

VERNE HARNISH:

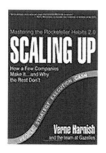

Scaling Up:
How a Few Companies Make It...and Why the
Rest Don't (Rockefeller Habits 2.0)
It's been over a decade since Verne Harnish's best-selling book *Mastering the Rockefeller Habits* was first released. *Scaling Up: How a Few Companies Make It... and Why the Rest Don't* is the first major revision of this business classic. In *Scaling Up*, Harnish and his team share practical tools and techniques for building an industry-dominating business. These approaches have been honed from over three decades of advising tens of thousands of CEOs and executives and helping them navigate the increasing complexities (and weight) that come with scaling up a venture. This book is written so everyone -- from frontline employees to senior executives -- can get aligned in contributing to the growth of a firm. There's no reason to do it alone, yet many top leaders feel like they are the ones dragging the rest of the organization up the S-curve of growth. The goal of this book is to help you turn what feels like an anchor into wind at your back -- creating a company where the team is engaged; the customers are doing your marketing; and everyone is making money. To accomplish this, *Scaling Up* focuses on the four major decision areas every company must get right: People, Strategy, Execution, and Cash. The book includes a series of new one-page tools including the updated One-Page Strategic Plan and the Rockefeller Habits ChecklistTM, which more than 40,000 firms around the globe have used to scale their companies successfully -- many to $1 billion and beyond. Running a business is ultimately about freedom. *Scaling Up* shows business leaders how to get their organizations moving in sync to create something significant and enjoy the ride.

VERNON MASON:

Don't Go!: A Practical Guide for Tackling Employee Turnover

Vernon Mason brings more than 24 years of experience as an early childhood administrator to the task of helping all kinds of organizations tackle the problem of high turnover. His practical strategies, tips, tactics, and suggestions will help any organization realize that to recruit and retain the best employees, you have to treat them right.

KRIS MURRAY'S
INSIDERS CIRCLE

WHO ELSE WANTS TO OVERCOME EVERY HURDLE THAT'S STANDING BETWEEN YOU AND A FULLY ENROLLED, PROFITABLE, AND SUCCESSFUL CHILD CARE PROGRAM?

As a Member of Kris Murray's Insiders Circle, with Access to Proven Strategies, Best Practices and Ongoing Support from CCMS & Fellow Members.

A private members-only community of early childhood business owners and leaders who meet together on the phone and online every month inside our private, members-only website to share success strategies, learn best practices and access all that the country's leading child care experts have to offer.

YOUR SUCCESS IS GUARANTEED!

KRIS MURRAY'S INSIDERS CIRCLE

SIGN UP AND GET A 30 MINUTE STRATEGY CALL WITH JESSICA!

Curious as to what part of being an "insider" is all about?

Have questions you'd like to ask Kris and Jessica live?

Could use a group of over 200 Early Childhood Educators at your fingertips for sharing advice and seeking answers?

As a thank you for reading my book, if you sign up for Kris Murray's Insider Circle (KMIC) for $49.97 per month………..

As a bonus for signing up and giving us a try, I will also offer you a complimentary 30-minute coaching call with me.

Kris Murray's Insider Circle is a monthly subscription and you can cancel at anytime (although most people don't)!

Too good to be true? I hope so. I want the opportunity to introduce myself to you live and hear about any issues that you are facing in Early Childhood Education. Also, growing our community is important to us. The more people in the child care industry that you have available to network with, the better. I wish I had such an amazing resource when I was working in a center.

HERE'S HOW YOU SIGN UP:

- Go to Childcare-marketing.com/jessicabookoffer

- Click on Buy Now – enter your information and click submit!

- That's it! We will then reach out to you to schedule your coaching call with me!